the Case of the Missing MOUNTAIN

by Kim Jones

Mystery rangers

Hi! I'm Mystery Ranger Jen. Welcome to an awesome ADVENTURE!

And I'm Mystery Ranger Jack! We have uncovered some ASTOUNDING MYSTERIES at Mount St. Helens in Washington State!

Help solve these mysteries and you can become an OFFICIAL MYSTERY RANGER.
A Mystery Ranger solves mysteries in nature by discovering clues, looking for evidence, and investigating!
You will be AMAZED as you explore the clues left behind by an event that changed this mountain forever.

A mountain is missing, and it's your job to find out how it could have disappeared to earn your Mystery Rangers badge!

Official Mystery Ranger Requirements:

1. **Solve all seven of the mysteries.**

2. **Complete at least two missions from the Mystery Ranger Mission List.**

3. **Complete at least two Rockin' Ranger Activities.**

First printing: January 2011
Second printing: May 2019

Copyright © 2011 by Kim Jones.
All rights reserved. No part of this book may be used or reproduced in any manner whatsoever without written permission of the publisher, except in the case of brief quotations in articles and reviews. For information write: Master Books®, P.O. Box 726, Green Forest, AR 72638.

Master Books® is a division of New Leaf Publishing Group, Inc.

ISBN 13: 978-0-89051-593-8
ISBN 13: 978-1-61458-503-9 (digital)
Library of Congress Number: 2010939347
Cover & Interior Design: Diana Bogardus
Jen and Jack Illustrations: Judah Fansler

Printed in China

Please visit our website for other great titles: www.masterbooks.com

For information regarding author interviews, please contact the publicity department at (870) 438-5288.

PHOTO CREDITS:

USGS pg 4, pg 6, pg 9, pg 10, pg 21, pg 22, pg 30, pg 35, pg 38, pg 41, pg 67, pg 58, pg 60, pg 72, Back Cover

US Forestry Service: pg 60

Portland State University Geology Dept: pg 8

Wiki: pg 12, pg 22

iStock.com: pg 19, pg 62, pg 63

shutterstock.com: pg 22, pg 24, pg 26, pg 27, pg 30, pg 33, pg 41, pg 44, pg 62, pg 63, pg 66, pg 67, Cover Image

Steven A. Austin: pg 28, pg 30, pg 41, pg 42, pg 52

Bryan Miller: pg 48

Tony Farley: pg 58,

E. Michael Kipp: pg 65

Official Mystery Ranger Rewards

There is a helpful checklist in the back to keep track of your progress. To download your reward and check your answers with the activity answer key, go to: thenaturetour.com

- **Official Mystery Ranger Certificate**
- **Official Mystery Ranger Badge**

Rangers Jack and Jen will both be your guides on this adventure.

WASHINGTON

▲ Mount Rainier

Mount St. Helens

▲ ▲ Mount Adams

The Mystery Begins!

1. The adventure starts here! Help find the way! Circle Mount St. Helens on the map.

2. Watch for clues! They will have the Mystery Ranger Symbol on them. Help solve the mystery and earn your Mystery Ranger badge and a chance to solve a challenge at the end of the case.

3. What is the abbreviation for Mount? ____ ____

4. What does St. in "Mount St. Helens" stand for? ____ ____ ____ ____ ____ ____

Mystery of the Vanishing Volcano

Mystery Clue 1 > Mount St. Helens was called Queen of the Cascade Mountains!

mystery ranger

Watch Out! There could be RDGANE! _ _ _ _ _ _ _
(unscramble this word)

Help us watch for clues! They'll be marked by a Mystery Ranger badge just like this one!

mystery ranger

Ranger Jack, I see an envelope with the symbol on it over by those rocks! Let's investigate! There are mystery clues inside the envelope! Let's open the first one!

hint

The mountain looks like a big bowl of ice cream! This is interesting! The clue says to watch out for something! Be careful! Let's go!

It's a picture of Mount St. Helens! Spirit Lake looks like a great place to fish! I can hardly wait to get there!

Ranger Jen, here's the second clue in the envelope.

What happened!

Mystery Clue 2 > Mount St. Helens USED to be a rockin' vacation spot! However, deep inside Mount St. Helens, DANGER was brewing!

"Danger!" How could this mystery be dangerous? What kind of TROUBLE was brewing at Mount St. Helens?

Looks like a great place for a vacation! Why did the clue say it USED TO BE a rockin' vacation spot?

DANGER!

MYSTERY DANGER: Find all 14 words in the mystery question below. Try to discover two extra clue words hidden in the puzzle.

[Mt. St. Helens] [used] [to] [be] [a] [vacation] [paradise]. [What] [happened] [to] [it]? [Beware] [of] [Danger]!

										M	V
					H	T	S	T			
S	N	E	L	E				W	H	A	T	O
D	A	N	G	E	R	W		D	D	F	L
H	A	P	P	E	N	E	D	A	W	E	B	C
F	Y	G	E	E	R		K	S	A	A
O	T	S	A	L	B	V		P	U	Q	N
E	S	I	D	A	R	A					
V	A	C	A	T	I	O	N	F	L	O

#1

5

Here is Mystery Clue 3 from the envelope! WHAT HAPPENED? The "After" picture looks like the moon, but the clue says it is Mount St. Helens.

Eye Spy!

What's missing? Use your detective skills. Circle at least three differences between the **before** and **after** pictures of Mount St. Helens.

Mystery Clue 3 > Before & After!

May 17, 1980

September 10, 1980

mystery ranger

This is Mount St. Helens just a few months later. It's not the moon!

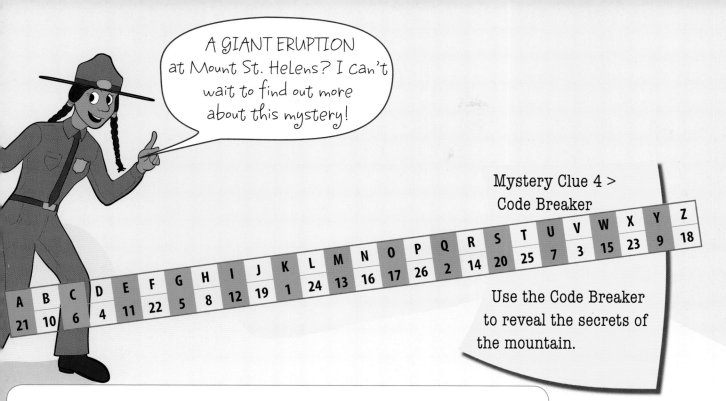

A GIANT ERUPTION at Mount St. Helens? I can't wait to find out more about this mystery!

Mystery Clue 4 > Code Breaker

A	B	C	D	E	F	G	H	I	J	K	L	M	N	O	P	Q	R	S	T	U	V	W	X	Y	Z
21	10	6	4	11	22	5	8	12	19	1	24	13	16	17	26	2	14	20	25	7	3	23	9	9	18

Use the Code Breaker to reveal the secrets of the mountain.

Danger lurked quietly under Mount St. Helens, a paradise of clear

_____ (24 21 1 11 20) and beautiful forests full of _____ (15 12 24 4 24 12 22 11)

Unaware of danger, people vacationed and worked on the mountain.

Mount St. Helens the next day? How could Mount St. Helens change that much SO QUICKLY? Help us solve this mystery!

Suddenly, Mount St. Helens woke up! Thousands of minor earthquakes signaled magma movement! Pushing with mighty force, magma created a giant _____ (10 7 24 5 11) 450 feet tall, near the top of the mountain on the _____ (16 17 14 25 8) side.

As the MONSTROUS bulge filled with fiery hot melted

rock called _____ (13 21 5 13 21), it grew. Snow and ice on top of the mountain melted and seeped into tiny

_____ (6 14 21 6 1 20) created by the minor earthquakes.

THE ERUPTION!
People were warned to leave the area before the eruption. Most did. Some did not.

7

You're doing good! Here are more clues to solve! Use the code breaker on pg. 7 to discover the clues on pg 8 & 9.

On May 18, 1980, a very powerful

11	21	14	25	8	2	7	21	1	11

shook Mount St. Helens, causing the north side bulge of the mountain to start to plunge into the valley below.

As the bulge slid off, SUPER HOT water inside the mountain exploded

to

20	25	11	21	13

causing the clay layers inside the mountain

to be very

20	24	12	26	26	11	14	9

.

ZOOM! ZOOM! ZOOM! In three sections, the bulge, along with the top one quarter, and then half of the mountain's insides slid off into the largest

24	21	16	4	20	24	12	4	11

in recorded history!

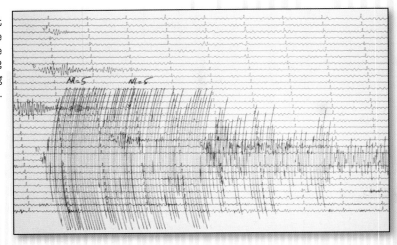

Richter scales measured the Mount St. Helens eruption at 5.1 on the morning of May 18, 1980. The violent explosion took place at 8:32 on a Sunday morning following weeks of ominous warning signs.

WHOOSH!

When the ground slid away, it was like shaking up a bottle of soda, and taking off the cap!

It released the ___ ___ ___ ___ ___ ___ ___ ___ inside the mountain with huge
     26 14 11 20 20 7 14 11

LATERAL (sideways) and VERTICAL **BLASTS!**

BOOM

In just ___ ___ ___ ___ ___ to ___ ___ ___ ___ MINUTES, most of the damage to the area
    25 8 14 11 11   22 17 7 14

was done! The mountain was disfigured beyond recognition. The valley was filled with the

landslide, and forest as large as a big ___ ___ ___ ___ were destroyed.
        6 12 25 9

The main eruption continued for ___ ___ ___ ___
        16 12 16 11
hours, forming an ash cloud over 12 miles high!

Mount St. Helens did not look like it did

before the eruption! The mountain and area

to the north looked like the surface of the

___ ___ ___ ___.
13 17 17 16

Wow! Scientists were AMAZED that SO MUCH land could be

changed SO ___ ___ ___ ___ ___ ___ ___.
      2 7 12 6 1 24 9

#1

9

Mount St. Helens was TOTALLY TRANSFORMED from quiet, beautiful forests to grey, lifeless-looking landscape in JUST THREE to FOUR MINUTES!

Decode the clues on the next page using the Mystery Decoder to discover which type of volcano has this SUPER speedy destructive power!

Is Mount St. Helens a shield or composite volcano?!

Lots of layers of **LAVA! LAVA! LAVA!**
Multiple lava flows build up to create the wide, gently sloping cone of a shield volcano. Most shield volcanoes erupt _____ – _____ This type of eruption

🐛 🦤 🐛   🦌 ✋ 🦔 🦙 🦤 🦎 🦎 🌋 🦌 🐗 🦬

can destroy _____ ,

🦔 🦝 🦤 🦔 🦌 🦝 🦡 🐗

but rarely causes death or injury. Mauna Loa volcano in Hawaii which rises over 30,000 feet above the ocean floor, is a shield volcano.

Shield Volcano

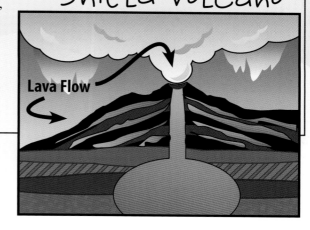

Lava Flow

Composite Volcano

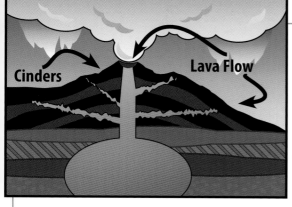

Cinders   Lava Flow

LAVA, ASH, AND ROCK FRAGMENT SANDWICH! Composite volcanoes, usually very steep and tall, are made of alternating layers of lava, ash, and rock fragments. They tend to erupt

🦌 ✋ 🦔 🦙 🦤 🦎 🦎 🌋 🦌 🐗 🦬

because the magma is too stiff for gasses to escape easily. Pressure builds as trapped gases expand until it is released in a violent eruption very _____ to

🦗 🦕 🐛 🦤 🦌 🦝 🦤 ☂ 🦎

people and property. Composite volcanoes are also known as stratovolcanoes. Mount Fuji in Japan is a composite volcano.

Mount St. Helens erupted explosively. It is a _____ Volcano.

🐺 🦤 🦘 🦔 🦤 🦎 🦎 🦡 🦌

Help the Mystery Rangers answer questions and solve this mystery by completing the CRATER CRISSCROSS on the next page. Search the word bank on pg. 13 and fill in the words below. The number before the word matches the number in Crater Criss Cross for clues.

Ah ha! There was an explosive eruption at 10.__ __ __ __ __ __ __ __ __ __ because it's a

2. __ . That's why there was a lot of 1.__ __ __ __ __ __!

Many scientists used to think this much change to a landscape took millions of years. But MOST of this change took just THREE to FOUR 6.__ __ __ __ __ __ __!

Did the volcano really 5. __ __ __ __ __ __? No, it was still there. But it looked TOTALLY different than before the 8. __ __ __ __ __ __ __ __ __ . It was no longer a vacation paradise. The HUGE debris avalanche left the mountain 1,314 feet shorter, with a HUGE horseshoe shaped 9.__ __ __ __ __ __ on top.

How far did the 3.__ __ __ __ __ reach? It reached up to 17 miles on the 7.__ __ __ __ __ side

The damage could be divided into three zones.

1. __ __ __ __(4)
Removal Zone
(No trees left)

2. __ __ __ __
__ __ __ __ (12) Zone
(Trees blown over)

3. __ __ __ __ __ __ __ __
(11) Zone (Trees were standing but scorched.)

Crater Criss Cross!

Wow! If one little volcano did so much damage so quickly, how much damage could Noah's Flood have done?!

Word Bank

Blast
Blowdown
Composite Volcano
Crater
Danger
Eruption
Minutes
Mt. St. Helens
North
Scorch
Tree
Vanish

A Warrior's Volcano

Build Your Own Mini Volcano!

Unscramble these words to discover what kind of gas is formed when baking soda and vinegar react.
(brCano xDoiedi)

C _ r _ _ n D _ _ x _ d _

 DIRECTIONS:

 This gas is found in real volcanoes!

Magma Messiness! Do this activity outside if you do not use a tray! This eruption of fun can be REALLY messy!

Magma Chamber Under Construction! Place bottle on tray or any surface where you would like to build your volcano.

Build-A-Cone! Mold clay, sand, or soil around bottle into a cone-shaped mountain.

Molten Magma! Use the funnel to pour in warm water, vinegar, detergent, and a few drops of food coloring.

Make a Bundle! Pour baking soda onto tissue. Wrap it up into a small bundle.

Eruption! Push the baking soda bundle into the bottle and STAND BACK! Watch your mini-volcano erupt!

 Why do you think this model is called a Warrior's Volcano? This type of volcano is shaped like something warriors carried to protect themselves in battle.

This volcano model represents a (dsiehl)

___ h ___ ___ ___ ___ volcano.

Make sure to have an adult help you!!

ROCKIN' RANGER

Volcano-On-the-Go!

Go on a mystery exploration to discover the perfect lava tub location! (Tub should NOT be made of granite, marble, tile, or slate.)

WARNING
Do NOT use lava mixture on stone surfaces such as marble, granite, tile, or slate!

½ cup baking soda
½ cup vinegar

Sponge
Bathtub

Mix up a Lagoon of Lava to fight scary scum!

Volcanic Mountain! Pour baking soda into the tub. Form baking soda into a mountain shape, with a crater in the middle.

Volcano Lava Flow! Pour vinegar into the baking soda crater to create an amazing "volcanic lava flow."

Lava Power versus Scum! Soap scum beware! Mix, whirl, and twirl "volcanic lava" around inside of tub, rubbing it on soap scum with the sponge. Scum may try to cling to the tub with all its might, but lava power will soon win out!

Lava Power to the Rescue! Turn on water to rinse the tub. Soap scum is all washed up!

Examine the Evidence! What happened when the vinegar and baking soda met? What did it do to the soap scum?

The steady lava flows from this type of eruption can build up into a shield volcano.

Unscramble the words in parantheses to solve this Mystery!

Magma, which is melted (rcko) _ _ _ **C** _ inside of a volcano, is called (aalv) _ _ **V** _ when it reaches the earth's (srfaceu) **S** _ **R** _ **A C** _ !

hint This experiment simulates the calmest of all eruptions, those that form a chain of islands, like a Hawaiian eruption.

ROCKIN' RANGER

Soda Blast Shake-up!

You need: Soft drink or soda water in a clear plastic bottle, scissors
This activity needs to have adult supervision.

Just cutting up! Cut the label off bottle.

Shake, shake, shake! Earthquake! Shake the bottle for 35 seconds!

Bubble Trouble! Inspect bubbles in the bottle. Where are the bubbles larger? Where are they smaller?

Get Ready! Point the bottle opening away from your face and anyone else with you!

Have a Blast! CAREFULLY open the bottle!

Examine the Evidence! Wow! What happened?

Fill in the blanks with words from the word bank to blast this bubble mystery!

WORD BANK
Pressure   Gas
Blast   Land
Trapped   Mountain

The bubbles in the bottle are like ___ ___ ___ bubbles rising out of the magma of a volcano. They are ___ ___ ___ P ___ ___ ___ against the lid, and the pressure builds.

When the cap was taken off the bottle, and the ___ ___ ___ S ___ ___ ___ ___ was released, what happened?

This is a great comparison to what happened at Mount St. Helens. When the ___ ___ N ___ slid off the top of the ___ ___ ___ ___ T ___ ___ ___, the pressure was released, and there was a gigantic ___ L ___ ___ ___!

Experience the Power

You need:
Empty Water Bottle (16 – 20 ounces)
1 to 2 sections of tissue   Funnel
1 tsp baking soda   8 drops dishwashing soap
1 cup vinegar

Make sure to have an adult help you!!

Molten Magma! Use the funnel to pour the vinegar and soap into the bottle.

Baking Soda Bundle! Pour baking soda onto tissue. Wrap it up into a small packet.

Eruption! Push the baking soda bundle into the bottle. Point the mouth of the bottle away from you. Quickly place your hand over the top of the bottle and shake it for 15 to 20 seconds!

Examine the Evidence! Something astonishing occurs! What happened?

Unscramble these words to unlock the secrets of this mystery!

All of these volcano models are a little different from real
(noeslovca) ___ ___ ___ ___ ___ N ___ E ___.

In this volcano model, (bonrac xdioeid) ___ ___ R B ___ ___
D ___ O ___ ___ ___ ___ caused the eruption.

In most volcanoes, (twrea vproa) W ___ ___ E ___ V ___ ___ ___ R is the main gas causing most eruptions, not carbon dioxide.

#1

mystery#2

Mystery of Exploding Ice & Snow

> I think I see something in that canyon! It might be a clue to our next mystery! I'm going down to investigate!

> Be careful, Ranger Jack! It looks very dangerous!

Hiking near Mount St. Helens is great! It's amazing how much damage the blast did in such a short time!

To discover which safety equipment Ranger Jack used to climb down into the canyon, cross out all of these letters from the grid: U, V, W, X, Y, Z

V W H U A Y R Z N X X E U S V S W A

N Z D X R Y O U P Z Z X E

_____

write it here

I found some clues! I'll bring them when I come back up from the canyon. This mystery is about ice and snow that EXPLODES!

Exploding ice and snow! This does sound dangerous!

Ranger Jack! Where are you?

What could possibly make snow and ice explode?

One hour later . . . Ranger Jack has not come back. Ranger Jen can't find him anywhere! Something must be wrong!

#2

19

Canyon Creation!

This canyon was formed two years after the "Big" eruption. It is called the "Little Grand Canyon." It is 100 feet deep and was formed in one day from a mudflow produced by a smaller eruption.

Help Mystery Ranger Jack escape from the canyon by guiding him through the maze!

Without your help, Ranger Jack could have been lost for a long time in that canyon!

Thanks for helping me escape the canyon. Let's take a look at the clues.

Crack the code to these EXPLOSIVE clues by rearranging the words that are backward!

Clue #1

EARTHQUAKE!

A huge earthquake caused (sedilsdnal) _ _ _ _ _ _ _ _ _ _ _ of rock, mud, ice, and snow to race down Mount St. Helens! The ice and snow were buried and trapped in the valley under the landslide.

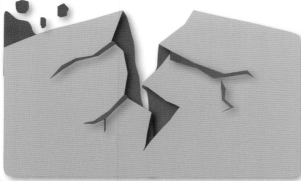

Clue #2

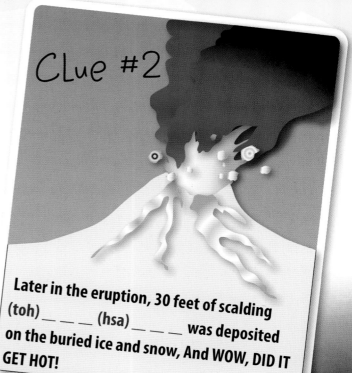

Later in the eruption, 30 feet of scalding (toh) _ _ _ (hsa) _ _ _ was deposited on the buried ice and snow, And WOW, DID IT GET HOT!

Clue #3

The buried ice and snow melted, flashing to (maets) _ _ _ _ _ , creating BIG (SNOISOLPXE) _ _ _ _ _ _ _ _ _ _ in _ _ _ _ _ _ _ _ _ _ _ _ _ the pumice plain, forming

STEAM EXPLOSION PITS!

Clue # 4

After the explosions, loose (ecimup) _ _ _ _ _ _ _ , on the rear-vertical sides of the pits tumbled down the sides to the bottom. This created an incredible feature in the pits called (sllir) _ _ _ _ _ and (seillug) _ _ _ _ _ _ _ (shallow and deep ditches) in JUST FIVE DAYS!

A close-up of pumice: see how the small chambers are formed when lava makes contact with water, heating the water, turning the lava hard almost instantly and trapping bubbles inside.

Clue #5

Rills and gullies are also a feature of a landform called (sdnaldab)

_ _ _ _ _ _ _ _ .

Badlands topography in the United States can be found in South Dakota and in the Southwest.

About three dozen steam explosion pits of varying sizes were identified.

 Gravity caused the pit walls to collapse.

Clue # 6

Badlands occur where rapid (noisore) _ _ _ _ _ _ has cut loose, dry soil or soft rocks into strange shapes. Badlands have lots of weird and wild looking (yratnemides) _ _ _ _ _ _ _ _ _ _ rock formations including rills, gullies, (selcannip) _ _ _ _ _ _ _ _ _ , spires and hoodoos.

Clue # 7

Badlands Recipe for Massive Erosion

➔ **Quick, intense (niar)** _ _ _ _ **storms**

➔ **Few (stnalp)** _ _ _ _ _ _

➔ **Soft (stnemides)** _ _ _ _ _ _ _ _ _

> Hmm, that's pretty fast, but at that rate it would take a long time for the Badlands to form.

Could they have formed quickly?

AVERAGE CURRENT RATES OF BADLANDS EROSION

Fragile rock layers = 1 inch per year

Sandstone = 1 inch per 500 years

TIME NEEDED TO CREATE EXPLOSION PITS WITH RILLS AND GULLIES

Explosion pit 125 feet deep = IMMEDIATELY when ice and snow exploded.

Rills and gullies = FIVE DAYS or less.

Clue # 8

Mount St. Helens Recipe for Massive Erosion

➔ **(cinaclov)** _ _ _ _ _ _ _ _ **eruption**

➔ **Steam (snoisolpxe)** _ _ _ _ _ _ _ _ _ _

➔ **(esool)** _ _ _ _ _ **sediments**

➔ **No (stnalp)** _ _ _ _ _ _

➔ **Pull of (ytivarg)** _ _ _ _ _ _ _

Clue #9 SOMETHING TO THINK ABOUT

Badlands topography covers HUGE areas.

What (ehportsatac) _ _ _ _ _ _ _ _ _ _ _ _ _ **would be large enough to cause this much massive erosion very quickly?**

> Wow! 125 feet of erosion with rills and gullies in 5 days is Super Speedy!

Clue #10

Steam Explosion Pit — Mount St. Helens

Clue #11

Badlands of South Dakota

Here are the last two clues in this mystery! Amazing! Look at these two pictures!

hint Both of these landforms look very much alike!

This evidence demonstrates that it did not have to take hundreds or thousands of years for the Badlands of South Dakota to form. Follow the evidence to discover the fascinating conclusions to this mystery! A code is used in this puzzle: 2 = A, 4 = B, 6= C, and so on.

This evidence demonstrates that it did NOT have to take

| | | | | | | | |
16 42 28 8 36 10 8 38

or ___ ___ ___ ___ ___ ___ ___ ___ ___ of ___ ___ ___ ___ ___ for the
40 16 30 42 38 2 28 8 38   50 10 2 36 38

___ ___ ___ ___ ___ ___ ___ ___ of South ___ ___ ___ ___ ___ ___ to form!
4 2 8 24 2 28 8 38   8 2 22 30 40 2

Mystery #2 Solved!

The Mystery Rangers need help unscrambling these words to explode this coded mystery!

Now I see how ice and snow can EXPLODE! Can we see the huge 125-foot explosion pit?

The back of the last clue says a couple of years later a mudflow cut through it, and it became part of a canyon! Let's go look for more clues!

The 5.1 earthquake at Mount St. Helens caused three (desllnaids) _ _ _ _ _ _ _ _ _ _ which joined together to form one giant landslide!

The giant landslide carried huge amounts of (eic) _ _ _ and (wons) _ _ _ _!

The buried ice and snow were covered with very hot volcanic (sah) _ _ _ _.

The buried ice and snow quickly flashed to (tmesa) _ _ _ _ _ _.

When the steam built up pressure too quickly it caused large (spoxelnsio) _ _ _ _ _ _ _ _ _ _!

These steam explosions created steam explosion (stpi) _ _ _ _.

The force of (ygatriv) _ _ _ _ _ _ _ helped carve rills and gullies into the sides of the pits.

The pumice plain now had huge pits, and looked similar to an area in South Dakota called the (dslBaand) _ _ _ _ _ _ _ _.

The steam explosion pits at Mount St. Helens looked like badlands topography in only (efvi) _ _ _ _ days.

#2

ROCKIN' RANGER

Slippery Slopes

Create your own Badlands: You need:
- 2 Baking Pans – rectangular or round
- Watering can or spray bottle & water
- 10 to 20 Popsicle or regular sticks
- Leaves and grass
- Dirt – Use to form two mountains 4 to 5 inches tall

Build a mountain! Fill pans with equal amounts of soil, forming a "mountain" on one end of each pan.

Mountain mover! Tilt pans up so the "mountain" is at the top of the pans.

Private eye spy sticks! Draw a line on the sticks, every ¼ inch.

Detective groundwork! Place 5–10 sticks randomly into each "mountain," burying them at least ½ inch deep.

The cover up! Cover the soil in one pan with broken-up leaves and grass.

The rain comes down! Pour water on both "mountains" from the watering can.

Examine the evidence!

> What happened?
> Inspect your sticks.
> Which "mountain" eroded faster? Why?
> Can you see any rills or gullies beginning to form?

It's fun to see how the water changes the shape of the "mountain" in this activity!

Water can shape a landscape. The question is how long does it really take?

Fill in the blanks with these words from the word bank to uncover the dirt on this mystery!

Water can wash away small amounts of soil, creating very small channels called ___ ___ L ___ ___.

If water continues to flow in rill channels, deeper ditches called ___ ___ ___ ___ ___ E ___ will form.

AMAZING! ___ ___ T ___ ___ erosion is usually what forms rills and gullies. HOWEVER, at Mount St. Helens, rills and gullies were formed by ___ ___ ___ A ___ explosions and ___ ___ A ___ ___ ___ ___ in just five days!

#2

The Wave at Coyote Buttes: Kanab, UT

mystery #3

Mystery of the Cliff of Secrets

Cliff of Secrets

March 19, 1982

June 12, 1980

March 18, 1980

1

2

3

Courtesy of Steve Austin

Look, Ranger Jack, I see an envelope at the bottom of that cliff! We have found the Cliff of Secrets!

This 60-foot cliff near Mount St. Helens has LOTS of thin layers! It also has three BIG (or MAJOR) sections. The bottom layer formed first.

Eye Spy!

Decode and answer this mystery question. Each letter in the question is coded as the next letter in the alphabet. Example: Volcano would be coded as Unkbzmn.

What scary secrets could this cliff hide? Investigate the clues!

(z = a, a = b, etc)

Gnv ezrs chc oxqnbkzrshb eknvr bqdzsd 200 kzxdqr ne sghr bkhee?

How long did it take to form the cliff? During a two-year period, three separate events formed the cliff.

I see the three major sections! From now on we'll call the sections by their scientific name: DEPOSITS.

Start reading the clues from the bottom first. Use this code to decipher these clues: 1 = A, 2 = B, and so on

Mighty Mud Secret #1

Created by melting snow from an eruption, this mighty

mudflow muscled its way down the mountain covering

and carving through past avalanche | | | | | | (4 5 2 18 9 19). Like icing on a cake, it covered the cliff of

secrets, forming the | | (20 15 16) deposit. You might say this section was **TOP SECRET!**

(Eruption — March 19, 1982)

Pyroclastic Power Secret #2

A raging HOT fiery cloud of gas, rocks, and ash called a | | | | | | | | | | | (16 25 18 15 3 12 1 19 20 9 3) flow

stormed at hurricane speed down the volcano, creating over 200 layers in just three hours!

Terrifying Tephra Secret #3

Volcanic lightening, triggered by swirling ash, flashed all around! Tephra (any kind of

| | | (1 19 8) and | | | | (18 15 3 11) ejected from a volcano through the air) spewed from Mt. St. Helens for

nine hours, creating this 30 foot deep deposit. (Eruption — May 18, 1980)

The Big Secret
The picture on page 28 shows only the top 60 feet of a 600 foot deposit! Below the third layer, is a 540-foot deposit of landslide debris that traveled ahead of the Tephra flow!

Mt. St. Helens

Amazing! Over 200 Layers were created at Mount St. Helens in JUST THREE HOURS by pyroclastic flows!

Do you recognize this layer? It is layer 2 of the Cliff of Secrets.

Courtesy of Steve Austin

Pyroclastic flow: Formed by super-fast flows of gas and rock.

Grand Canyon

Wow! The layering in these two cliffs looks very similar!

hint Some geologists think layers of rock, like this Tapeats Sandstone at the Grand Canyon, were formed over millions of years by slow moving water. HOWEVER. . . .

Follow the evidence to discover the fascinating conclusions to this mystery! A code is used in this puzzle. Count by 5: 5 = A, 10 = B and so on.

Tapeats Sandstone, Grand Canyon
Formed by super fast flows of water and rock.

30 60 75 75 20   35 25 75 60 75 35 45 95 100 95   suspect the

100 5 80 25 5 100 95   60 5 125 25 90 95   at the   35 90 5 70 20   15 5 70 125 75 70

were formed during   70 75 5 40 95   30 60 75 75 20   !

Use your detective skills to find the secret words!

mystery ranger

TOP SECRET WORD LIST!

CLUE	MUDFLOW
GEOLOGIST	PYROCLASTIC
CLIFF	MOUNT ST HELENS
QUICK	EXPLOSION
FLOOD	SANDSTONE
SECRET	GRAND CANYON
LAYERS	THREE HOURS
ASH	VOLCANO

```
S  N  Y  L  T  T  I  J  R  F  B  F  F  E  M  D  X
R  A  O  O  O  E  G  E  N  N  F  E  A  O  H  A  Y
U  G  J  Y  I  Z  R  Y  F  I  R  R  U  O  R  S  P
O  X  E  W  N  V  D  C  L  N  T  N  Q  Z  Q  R  J
H  F  I  O  L  A  V  C  E  H  T  O  Q  D  H  E  T
E  T  L  C  L  Q  C  I  T  S  A  L  C  O  R  Y  P
E  H  N  O  T  O  M  D  T  A  E  G  C  X  U  A  O
R  D  H  G  O  U  G  H  N  O  K  I  R  F  B  L  F
H  O  V  S  D  D  E  I  B  A  N  G  E  N  L  T  Z
T  G  V  F  A  L  Z  I  S  O  R  T  A  B  A  U  I
O  N  L  K  E  D  N  R  I  T  U  G  T  H  S  K  L
K  O  B  N  M  D  Z  S  R  P  D  C  I  G  T  R  X
W  H  S  J  F  U  O  O  N  A  C  L  O  V  H  U  I
O  O  H  W  X  L  Z  C  S  F  B  A  N  K  S  X  N
E  W  C  H  P  Q  U  I  C  K  B  U  A  U  D  F  I
M  H  K  X  W  O  C  T  M  B  A  C  J  V  Q  S  Q
F  J  E  F  Z (S  A  N  D  S  T  O  N  E) U  L  C
```

Create a Color Crazy Cliff

ROCKIN' RANGER

You need:
Salt or sand
Food coloring
Plastic zipper seal bags
Clear glass or plastic water bottle with a lid
Funnel or rolled up paper
Measuring cup

Optional:
Paraffin wax
Pencil, or toothpick

Bag It! Pour 1/4 cup salt or sand into each bag (1 bag per color).

Capture the Colors! Pick your colors. Add 2 to 8 drops of food coloring per bag. Seal bags tightly. (Mix colors too!)

This activity represents pyroclastic flows forming over 200 layers in just three hours.

Shake, Rattle, & Roll! Shake and "smush" bag until color is well mixed through salt/sand. Add more food coloring if color is too light. (Pour salt/sand onto paper towels if it needs to dry.)

Pyroclastic Flow! Pour colored salt/sand through funnel into the bottle, one color layer at a time!

Note: This activity shows different layers that you create. In a real pyroclastic flow, different size particles self-sort by gravity so the largest are at the bottom.

Just for Fun! To make cool designs in your layers, stick a pencil or toothpick through the sand to create patterns.

Seal the Deal! Fill jar completely to top and close.

Pyroclastic Peanut Butter!

Pyroclastic Players Race to Create "Rock Layers!"
You Need:

- 1 to 2 packages of crackers (per team)
- Table or bench
- Crunchy peanut butter
- 2 Paper plates (1 per team)
- 2 large spoons (1 per team)

> Each team represents a pyroclastic flow from a volcano. We'll find out which flow is the fastest!

Directions:

Pyroclastic players! Divide players into two teams, forming two relay lines. Each line should face the table, leaving several feet of running space between teams and the table. Place a paper plate on the table for each team, along with peanut butter, crackers, and spoons.

Eruption! Play begins when the leader yells, "Eruption!"

Pyroclastic flow! First player in each team runs to the table, spreads peanut butter on the plate, adds one cracker layer, runs back, and tags the next person. On their turns, the rest of the players add peanut butter to the top cracker and add another cracker, forming peanut butter/cracker layers.

Lots of Layers! Team with the tallest stack of cracker pyroclastic layers in three minutes has the fastest flow!

Unscramble these words to go with the flow and solve this mystery.

A hot, fast-moving mixture of (sha) __ __ __, pumice, (rcko) R __ __ __ fragments, and gas formed during explosive eruptions is called a (citsalcoryp) P __ __ __ __ __ __ S __ __ __ flow.

Pyroclastic flows can travel as fast as 450 miles per hour!

The word PYROCLASTIC , comes from the Greek word *pyro* meaning (rife) __ __ R E and *klastos* meaning (nebokr) B __ __ K __ N.

Mystery of the Menacing Mudslinger

This mystery is about a menacing mudslinger.

Look! I found another secret decoder and more clues!

Use the secret decoder to solve the Mystery!

mystery ranger

secret decoder

A	B	C	D	E	F	G	H	I
J	K	L	M	N	O	P	Q	R
S	T	U	V	W	X	Y	Z	

There was a _____ here!

34

A giant slip-n-slide!

During the huge eruption of Mount St. Helens in 1980, the MASSIVE landslide triggered by the earthquake raced down the mountain at speeds up to 150 miles per hour! Hitting a ridge on its way down the mountain, the landslide was divided.

Part of the landslide (about 25 percent) slammed into

Hot ash from the eruption covered the landslide, causing ice and snow mixed in the slide to melt!

The rest of the landslide (75 percent) pushed and shoved its way through the valley, covering up 14 miles of the North Fork of the

About five hours after the blast began, the menacing mudslinger mudflow was born!

Melting ice and snow flowed rapidly over the landslide, gobbling up rocks, and trees from the landslide…

The menacing mudflow roared down the valley, snatching up everything in its path! Huge piles of cut

were sucked into the muddy mass when it smashed into logging camps.

Tumbling, smashing, and rolling, nothing stood in its way! It snapped steel bridges, crushed and buried houses, and tossed cars, busses, and trucks like they were toys.

#4

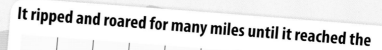

It ripped and roared for many miles until it reached the

River where it

settled down as a humongous mud pie, filling the river channel with so much mud that it was too shallow for big boats.

Eye Spy!

Leaving a deposit of deep mud and destruction everywhere it went, the menacing mudslinger's trail was easy to follow!

It destroyed 200 homes, 27 bridges, 185 miles of roads, and 15 miles of railroad track.

Hmm, with no way for water to escape, it sounds like Spirit Lake is getting deeper and deeper! If it floods, the people living downstream will be in lots of danger!

An Easy Journey!

Before the eruption, water could flow efficiently from the mountain to the sea! It could flow from:

▷ Mount St. Helens

▷ Spirit Lake

▷ North Fork of the Toutle River

◁ Other Rivers

◀ Pacific Ocean

For about two years after the eruption, it was much harder for water to flow from Mount St. Helens to the sea! If water flowed from Mount St. Helens into Spirit Lake, it was trapped! The exit for water was buried under the landslide! TO FLOW TO THE SEA, water had to flow for MILES over the bumpy landslide to the Toutle River, then down other rivers to the sea.

DANGER

Help these water droplets find their way from the volcano's crater, over the landslide, to the Toutle River, which goes into other rivers that lead to the Pacific Ocean. Watch for hazards to avoid disaster on the trip!

Swallowed by an elk!

Evaporated into the Sky!

Ooops! Slid into a pond.

Trapped behind a huge mound of rock.

Waterfall

Toutle River! This way to the Pacific Ocean!

After the 1980 eruption, for water to get from Mount St. Helens to the sea it had to travel over the rugged landscape of the landslide. That was until two years later when the March 19, 1982 mighty mudflow was born.

Have no fear! MIGHTY MUDFLOW is here! With a quake and shake, another eruption melted ⬜|⬜|⬜|⬜ in the crater of Mount St. Helens, and a SECOND HUGE MUDFLOW was born.

The MIGHTY MUDFLOW thundered down the mountain with speed, power, and lot's of mud. It was 20 miles long and ready to pack a punch through the lumpy landslide on the

However — something very mysterious and astonishing happened when the MIGHTY MUDFLOW surged over the landslide.

Why was this mudflow so mysterious?

Mudflow March 19, 1982

38

VICTORY FOR MIGHTY MUDFLOW! The landslide held its ground, but very quickly MIGHTY MUDFLOW swept away massive amounts of jumbled ____ ____ ____ ____ , ____ ____ ____ and dirt!

That sounds like erosion. What's mysterious and strange about that?

 **Erosion: Moving rocks or soil from one place to another.**

Geologists thought it would take many years for a "dendritic" river system like this one to form! All across the landslide, MIGHTY MUDFLOW eroded many small streams that connected to larger streams that flowed into the Toutle River. However, Mighty Mudflow carved a COMPLETE RIVER SYSTEM in JUST NINE HOURS!

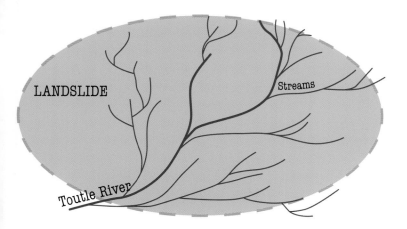

LANDSLIDE

Streams

Toutle River

Dendritic River System: Small streams flowing into larger streams and then to the river. It resembles a tree branch, lying across Mount St. Helens and the landslide!

A river system formed in JUST NINE HOURS? That is amazing!

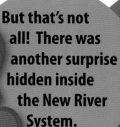 But that's not all! There was another surprise hidden inside the New River System.

Maybe we should go down into that canyon to search for more clues.

Wow! These canyons are deep! Come and see this!

A DEEP DISCOVERY! As scientists explored the new river system, they made an astounding discovery! The MIGHTY MUDFLOW had used its super erosion powers and carved a | | | | | in the new river system that was 140 feet deep in JUST **9** HOURS!

It was nicknamed "The Little | | | | Canyon" Because it appeared to be 1/40th the size of the Grand Canyon in Arizona!

hint

Little Grand Canyon was formed by rapid erosion. Could the Grand Canyon have been formed in a similar way?

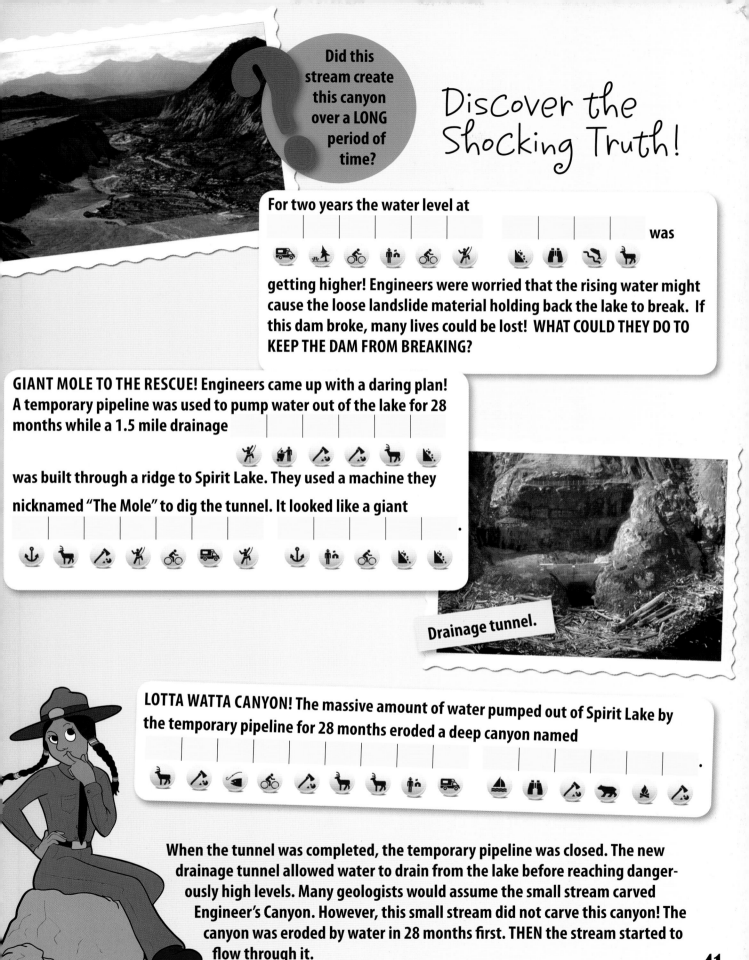

Did this stream create this canyon over a LONG period of time?

For two years the water level at _____ ____ was getting higher! Engineers were worried that the rising water might cause the loose landslide material holding back the lake to break. If this dam broke, many lives could be lost! **WHAT COULD THEY DO TO KEEP THE DAM FROM BREAKING?**

GIANT MOLE TO THE RESCUE! Engineers came up with a daring plan! A temporary pipeline was used to pump water out of the lake for 28 months while a 1.5 mile drainage _____ was built through a ridge to Spirit Lake. They used a machine they nicknamed "The Mole" to dig the tunnel. It looked like a giant _____ _____ .

Drainage tunnel.

LOTTA WATTA CANYON! The massive amount of water pumped out of Spirit Lake by the temporary pipeline for 28 months eroded a deep canyon named _____ _____ .

When the tunnel was completed, the temporary pipeline was closed. The new drainage tunnel allowed water to drain from the lake before reaching dangerously high levels. Many geologists would assume the small stream carved Engineer's Canyon. However, this small stream did not carve this canyon! The canyon was eroded by water in 28 months first. THEN the stream started to flow through it.

Little Grand Canyon

Engineer's Canyon

mystery ranger

Amazing! Engineer's Canyon was eroded by WATER in ONLY 28 months!

Even more amazing . . . the North Fork of the Toutle River System and the Little Grand Canyon were carved by a MUDFLOW in ONLY nine hours!

Wow! If a geologist didn't know the story of how fast these canyons formed, he/she might think they took a LONG time to form! However, these canyons formed VERY QUICKLY through the power of erosion!

This shows that landforms CAN form VERY quickly in catastrophes like Mount St. Helens! The mudflows at Mount St. Helens were both menacing (harmful) and mighty (helpful)!

HOW LONG DID IT TAKE THESE LANDFORMS TO DEVELOP?
Engineer's Canyon _____
Little Grand Canyon _____
North Fork Toutle River System _____

A City Is in Danger! Save It from a Monster Mudflow

WARNING
Adult supervision needed when cutting the bottles!

Help us stop the Monster Mudflow!

You Need:
2 empty plastic water bottles
Small trowel , shovel, or spoon
 Natural materials (leaves, twigs, etc.)

Scissors or knife
Bucket of water
Sloped area

Directions:

Spy Gear! Cut tops off bottles. Cut four small holes in bottom of ONE bottle.

Spy Eyes! Use your detective powers of observation to discover the perfect outdoor location — a sloped area.

Digging In! Dig a ditch on the slope (2–3 feet long and 2–3 inches deep).

The City! Place bottle with holes in bottom into ditch on its side, 4 inches above end of ditch, opening facing top of ditch. This is the city. Name the city.

The "Flood"! Fill the other bottle with water. This is the "flood."

EMERGENCY! Danger! Monster Mudflow is coming! Hold city in place. Starting at the top of the ditch, pour water from the "flood" down through the city. Lift city up. How much mud is in the city? Carefully dump mud out. (You don't want to injure the people!) Place city back in ditch.

Monster Mudflow! Must Be Stopped! How can you stop the Monster Mudflow from reaching the city? You may use natural materials such as leaves or twigs, to build some kind of structure in the ditch that stops mud from getting in the city, but allows water to flow through. (Be sure not to use poison ivy leaves!)

City Saver Super Hero! Test the structure as many times as needed until most of the mud is stopped. Congratulations! You are a Super Hero! You have saved the city!

#4

The Mystery of the Floating Forest

Petrified tree at Yellowstone

A floating forest! Petrified trees? What scared them?

The Mystery at Yellowstone! In Yellowstone National Park at "Specimen Ridge," scientists THOUGHT they had solved the mystery of 27 layers of petrified trees found buried in the mountainside! Some trees were standing up (vertical) and some were lying down (horizontal) in these layers.

Clue #1

How does the floating forest mystery at Mount St. Helens help explain the petrified trees at Yellowstone?

Scientists thought that 50 million or so years ago, there were up to 27 different forests growing in this location. They thought the trees took 20,000 years to petrify and be preserved in the mountainside. They put up a sign to explain their ideas.

Clue #2

Nothing scared them. Petrified trees are trees that have been changed into rock!

hint Because of what happened when Mount St. Helens erupted, the sign at Yellowstone had to be taken down. Let's see why!

Log Clues:

There are more clues floating on those logs in the lake!

① A 5.1 EARTHQUAKE causes a GIANT landslide at Mount St. Helens!

② Eruption! A sideways blast flattens the forest!

③ Part of a landslide crashes into Spirit Lake, triggering an 860-foot wave!

④ Over one million trees get washed into the lake by the giant wave!

⑤ Many trees floating on the lake rub together and lose their bark! They form a mat that covers the lake.

⑥ Trees become waterlogged. Some tilt upward because of heavy roots. The trees begin sinking at various times.

⑦ Trees sink according to type, some in a vertical (upright) position and others horizontally!

⑧ Sediment such as ash, rocks and soil wash into the lake, burying trees on the bottom a little at a time.

⑨ More trees sink! More sediment covers them.

⑩ And in just a few years the layering in Spirit Lake looks the same as that found at Yellowstone National Park!

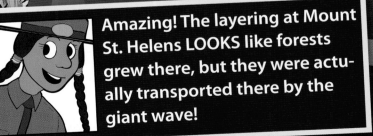

Amazing! The layering at Mount St. Helens LOOKS like forests grew there, but they were actually transported there by the giant wave!

The Secrets of Spirit Lake

Help Mystery Rangers Jen and Jack solve the mystery using the log clues to put the pictures in order. Write the correct clue number in the box by the picture in the order events occurred:

1. Earthquake causes giant landslide.
2. Eruption! Trees knocked over by blast.
3. Giant wave sweeps over land.
4. Wave carries trees to water.
5. A mat of trees form on the surface.
6. Trees at various times sink to the bottom.
7. Sediment buries trees on the bottom.
8. More trees sink and get covered by dirt and debris, forming layers.

Even though the trees were knocked down at the same time, the logs are being buried on the lake bottom at different times and levels! Does this look like the layering found at Yellowstone?

What did it look like under Spirit Lake after the blast?

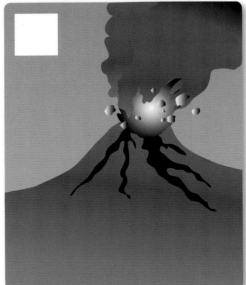

46

SOLVING THE SECRET

Dr. Steve Austin, a very brave geologist, dove with scuba gear, under Spirit Lake after the eruption. It was very dangerous because logs were sinking all around him. He discovered the upright trees sinking and being buried in layers on the bottom of the lake. He researched his ideas and discovered the connection between layering in Spirit Lake at Mount St. Helens and layering at Specimen Ridge in Yellowstone. He wrote several books about his amazing discoveries.

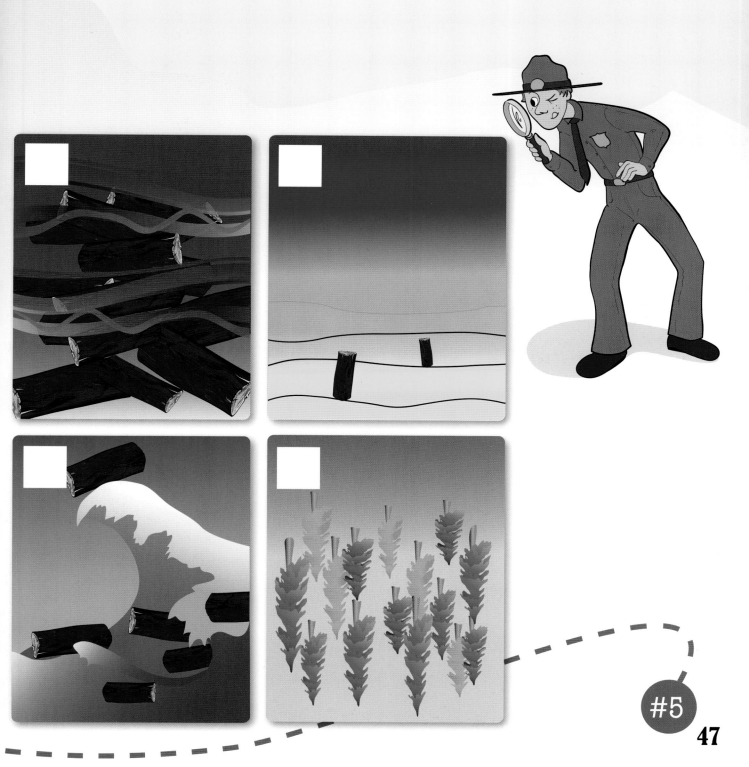

#5

47

What are growth rings in trees?

A tree's age can be estimated by counting the number of "growth rings." Each year of a tree's life there is one light and one dark ring for most trees. Together these form a growth ring that can also give clues about climate, disasters, or disease that might have occurred during the tree's life.

If a scientist compared growth rings from all these trees, he or she would be able to tell they all lived at the same time.

Some trees on Spirit Lake are still sinking to the bottom forming layers.

How long did this tree live? Count the growth rings on this tree to estimate its age. Circle the tree's scars. What do you think might have caused the scars?

Estimated age of tree _____

A series of 27 layers of petrified trees in Yellowstone National Park were thought to be 27 different forests that grew there and were buried by volcanic eruptions. However, due to new evidence provided by the eruption of Mount St. Helens, scientists studied the growth rings in the petrified trees at Yellowstone! They discovered that the trees in Specimen Ridge did live at the same time!

hint Dr. Harold Coffin made this discovery before the eruption. The eruption confirmed his work —one forest carried somewhere else by a series of mudflows.

Wow! Mystery solved! Because the trees were not 27 different forests, Yellowstone took down the sign! Discover petrification for yourself!

A Petrifying Demonstration!

A Model to Demonstrate the Process of Petrification!

You Need:

2 –3 cups clean sand
Plastic wrap
3 rubber bands
Water (room temperature)

Food coloring (2–4 colors)
6 clear cups
1 popsicle stick
6 small pieces of wood or freshly broken twigs (about 1 inch long each)

Petrified wood is a fossil that used to be wood! Wood can be petrified when it is buried in an area with hot water that has lots of silica (a mineral) in it — like Yellowstone National Park!
The mineral water soaks into the wood and removes or replaces the living part of the wood with silica. It makes a copy of the wood! Wood does not have to take long to petrify! In Yellowstone Park, roots and lower trunks of some trees are starting to be petrified while they are still alive!

Directions:

1. Fill 3 cups ¼ full of sand.

2. Place two pieces of wood in each cup on top of the sand.

3. Pour sand over the wood in each cup until it is covered. Cup will be about half full.

4. Fill three empty cups half full of water.

5. Using a different color for each cup, add 12 drops food color to each half cup of water. Stir.

6. Pour colored water SLOWLY into each sand cup. Cover sand totally, with just a tiny bit of water on top.

7. Wood should still be buried. If not, use the popsicle stick to re-bury it.

8. Cover three cups of sand with plastic wrap. Place rubber band tightly around cup.

9. Allow cups to sit for one week.

10. Take plastic wrap off cups. Are there any changes in the wood? Break the wood open and look inside for changes, too. What happened to the wood?

11. Just for fun! Try other objects besides wood, such as chicken bones, and see what happens!

mystery #6

Mystery of the Mighty Canyon Carvers!

Survival Supplies

Discover what survival supplies Ranger Jack and Jen have in their backpacks.
Use your detective skills to spy the hidden words in this puzzle.

Bandana
Bible
Binoculars
Camera
Compass
First aid kit

Flashlight
Food
Insect repellent
Jacket
Map
Mirror

Rope
~~Sunscreen~~
Water
Matches
Whistle

Clues to the next mystery are found in Step Canyon. It's up on the mountain, just below the crater.

```
P  M  T  W  U  N  F  Y  E  K  T  C  S  M  Q  B
B  I  B  L  E  B  W  N  F  H  L  O  R  X  J  R
U  V  S  B  N  J  H  A  G  H  H  M  A  Z  X  G
T  H  E  Y  E  D  P  I  T  W  Q  P  L  Q  J  X
H  I  O  B  O  U  L  A  H  E  T  A  U  G  E  Y
K  X  K  F  A  H  T  I  M  S  R  S  C  R  S  V
B  Q  O  D  S  N  S  E  I  B  P  S  O  O  U  T
L  O  N  A  I  T  D  R  K  O  E  P  N  R  S  M
D  J  L  G  L  A  H  A  N  C  T  U  I  R  P  A
Y  F  I  E  W  C  T  H  N  G  A  N  B  I  G  T
N  P  J  E  P  O  R  S  E  A  R  J  W  M  W  C
T  N  E  L  L  E  P  E  R  T  C  E  S  N  I  H
S  U  N  S  C  R  E  E  N  I  X  X  B  N  I  E
A  R  E  M  A  C  P  F  X  A  F  H  F  T  B  S
```

Being close to a volcano can be very dangerous! We have water and supplies in case of an emergency.

50

Help Ranger Jen and Ranger Jack find clues to the "Mystery of the Mighty Canyon Carvers," by solving this maze! Watch for danger!

Courtesy of Steve Austin

It looks like the waterfall comes from melting snow in the crater. There's a clue envelope by the waterfall!

Watch out! There's a rock slide! This area under the crater is very unstable. There could be another slide any minute.

DANGER

Hazardous rock slides are very common near the crater of Mount St. Helens. Unscramble the clues to discover some causes of these slides. (Check out the silly hints next to the words for an extra hint!)

seeatqhkrua
(I'm all shook up!)

_ _ _ _ _ h _ _ _ _ _ _ _

irenghaewt
(You crack me up!)

_ _ _ t _ _ _ i _ _ _

gwionrg alav eomd
(Hat for a volcano)

g _ _ w _ _ g l _ _ _ _ _ _ m _

eci wnso esplolac
(BRRRRRRRR! I'm falling!)

_ _ _ or _ _ _ _ _ _ c _ _ l _ p _ _ _

52

I opened the envelope but the answers to the clues are missing. This mystery is about some Mighty Canyon Carvers!

Moon Alphabet

Solve the clues of the Mystery of the Mighty Canyon Carvers by using this code. Use the moon alphabet code on the next three pages.

A	B	C	D	E	F
∧	∪	⊂	⊃	Γ	⌐

G	H	I	J	K	L
⌐	●	I	J	<	L

M	N	O	P	Q	R
⌐	N	O	⊂	⊐	/

S	T	U	V	W	X
/	—	∪	V	∩	>

Y	Z	AND	THE	!	?
⌐	Ζ	⊂	⋮	!	⌐

 This code was developed to be used by people who could not see. It is similar to braille. It was created by William Moon, so it was called "moon writing."

I can't see any writing, but I can feel some raised letters on the paper! Feels like a raised letter code called, "moon writing!" The moon alphabet can be read by touch!

Use the Moon Alphabet on page 53 to solve the clues below.

Two mysterious canyons formed near the mouth of the crater after the eruption of Mount St. Helens:

⬜⬜⬜⬜ ⬜⬜⬜⬜⬜⬜ **and**
_ _ _ _   C A N Y O N

⬜⬜⬜⬜⬜ ⬜⬜⬜⬜⬜⬜⬜
L O O _ _ _   C A N Y O N

Were these canyons formed by the Mighty Canyon Carvers?

These two canyons amazed geologists because they were formed in only

⬜⬜⬜⬜ ⬜⬜⬜⬜⬜⬜ !
_ I V _   _ O N _ _ _

⬜⬜⬜⬜⬜⬜⬜⬜
_ U _ _ _ _ O _ _

⬜⬜⬜⬜⬜⬜⬜⬜⬜⬜⬜⬜ ⬜⬜⬜⬜⬜
_ _ _ O C L A _ _ I C   _ _ O _ _

and water eroded and carved these canyons VERY quickly!

Amazing! The Mighty Canyon Carvers are fast, but who or what are they?

Ah ha! We have discovered the Mighty Canyon Carvers!

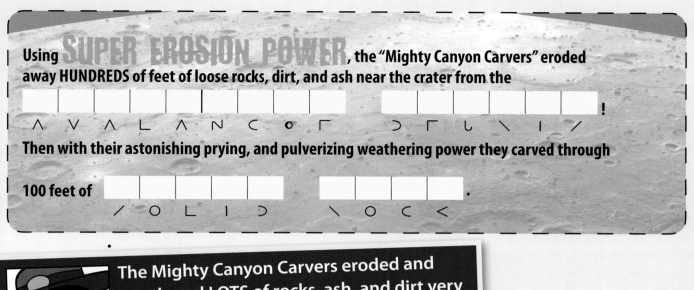

Using **SUPER EROSION POWER**, the "Mighty Canyon Carvers" eroded away HUNDREDS of feet of loose rocks, dirt, and ash near the crater from the

A V A L A N C H E   D E B R I S !

Then with their astonishing prying, and pulverizing weathering power they carved through

100 feet of

S O L I D   R O C K .

The Mighty Canyon Carvers eroded and weathered LOTS of rocks, ash, and dirt very quickly! They are POWERFUL! I want to see Loowit Canyon too. Let's keep decoding these clues using the moon alphabet!

hint

Erosion: Moving rocks and soil from one place to another.
Weathering: Breaking down of rocks into smaller pieces.

It took the super powered "Mighty Canyon Carvers" only

F I V E   M O N T H S

to carve Step Canyon 700 feet deep!

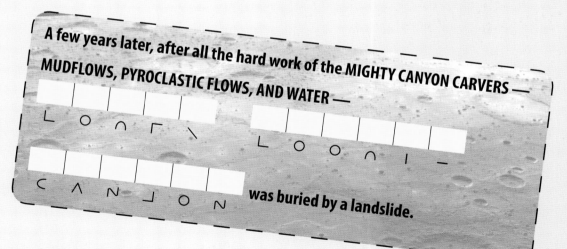

A few years later, after all the hard work of the MIGHTY CANYON CARVERS — MUDFLOWS, PYROCLASTIC FLOWS, AND WATER —

L O W E R   L O O W I T

C A N Y O N   was buried by a landslide.

Lower Loowit Canyon was buried, but you can still see Loowit Waterfall. The erosion and weathering Canyon Carvers have LOTS of work to do to dig it out again!

#6

55

Some geologists think the hard rock erosion of the canyons was caused by

C A V I _ A _ I O N and _ L U C K I N _

Cavitation: When water flows faster than 20 miles per hour, bubbles form that contain a vacuum (no air). These bizarre bubbles have crushing strength! When the bubbles EXPLODE inwardly, they make a noise like firecrackers and produce a SHOCK-WAVE of water able to smash and pound the rocks below them to pieces. This is called cavitation.

Plucking: Water flowing very quickly over rock can rip up loose blocks of bedrock and move them. This is called plucking. As the bedrock moves, it can crush the other rocks in its path.

Bizarre Bursting Bubbles!

A Game to Create Bizarre Bubble Art!

WARNING
Massively Messy! Outdoor activity! Wear old clothes, and stay away from houses!

You Need:

Bubble solution
Tempera or poster paint (3–4 colors)
3 to 4 small bowls
Teaspoon

Bubble wand or straw
Light-colored construction paper
Old clothes to wear!
Measuring cup

Directions:

Get Ready! Pour 1 cup of bubble solution into each bowl.

Just add color! Add 1 teaspoon of paint to each bowl. (Use a different color in each bowl.) Gently mix. Bubbles will be stronger if you stir slowly. To make colors darker, add more paint.

Bizarre Bubble Artist Game!
Artist: Dip bubble wand into solution and blow bubbles.
Bubble Snatcher: Bubble Snatcher tries to catch as many bubbles as possible on the page!

Bubble Art! When the bubbles break, splashes of color create a cool piece of artwork!

Note: Best done on a day when it's not windy!

mystery #7

Mystery of the Green Scene Machine

Clue # 1 – 1981

Clue # 2– 2009

mystery ranger

What changed this scene from gray to green? How did it change so fast?

hint
The first picture was taken soon after Mount St. Helens erupted.

The first picture is so gray with no plants

The second picture has lots of plants—just a few years later!

Square Code was used in World War II. Every word in square code has the letters A E I N T.

Hike through the Hummocks and you will see another clue to this _____ | _____ | _____ | _____ | _____ | _____ | _____

AI · IN · TA · AE · EE · NE · IN

Square Code

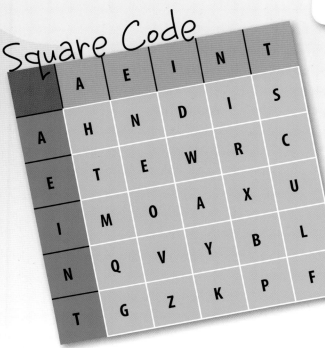

	A	E	I	N	T
A	H	N	D	I	S
E	T	E	W	R	C
I	M	O	A	X	U
N	Q	V	Y	B	L
T	G	Z	K	P	F

To read the code:

1. Find the first letter in the code on the top line. Put your finger on it.

2. Find the second letter in the code on the left vertical side. Put your finger on it.

3. The point where those two lines meet will be the code letter.

4. The letter J is always coded by a single I. I = J

Example: AT = G EI = O IA = D

The first letter always starts at the top. Use this code to solve the clues in Mystery 7 on pages 59, 60, 63–65.

Hike through Hummocks? What are Hummocks?

Here's a sign for the Hummocks Trail. Let's follow it to see if we can discover more clues.

Hummocks Trail »

#7

Toutle River Valley, 1983

The trail goes to the Toutle River Valley.

Toutle River Valley several years later

The

TN	II	EA	IA	TA	TN	NA	IA	EE

surged with SUPER SPEED 14 miles down the North Fork of the Toutle River. It filled the valley to an average thickness of 150 feet.

It is so green here! Did the volcano damage reach this far? I see another clue envelope!

Mounds of rock from the volcano, called

AA	TI	AI	AI	EI	TE	IT	TA

stick up like huge beached whales in the landslide deposit.

Survivors & Colonizers

Hidden below the damage from the eruption were secret survivors. After the eruption, colonizing plants and animals moved into the blast zone too. See if you can complete the puzzle using their names.

pocket gopher
beetle
spider
salamander
hemlock pine cones

lupine
fireweed
deer mouse
chipmunk
western toad

These plants and animals are called SURVIVORS and Colonizers.

Survivors and Colonizers helped change Mt. St. Helens from gray to green. Scientists were shocked to discover that some plants and animals survived the blast, like ants, deer mice, and pocket gophers! They were even more shocked at the "eruption" of life that followed very quickly afterward! Scientists are closely studying the return of life.

pocket gopher

deer mouse

ant

61

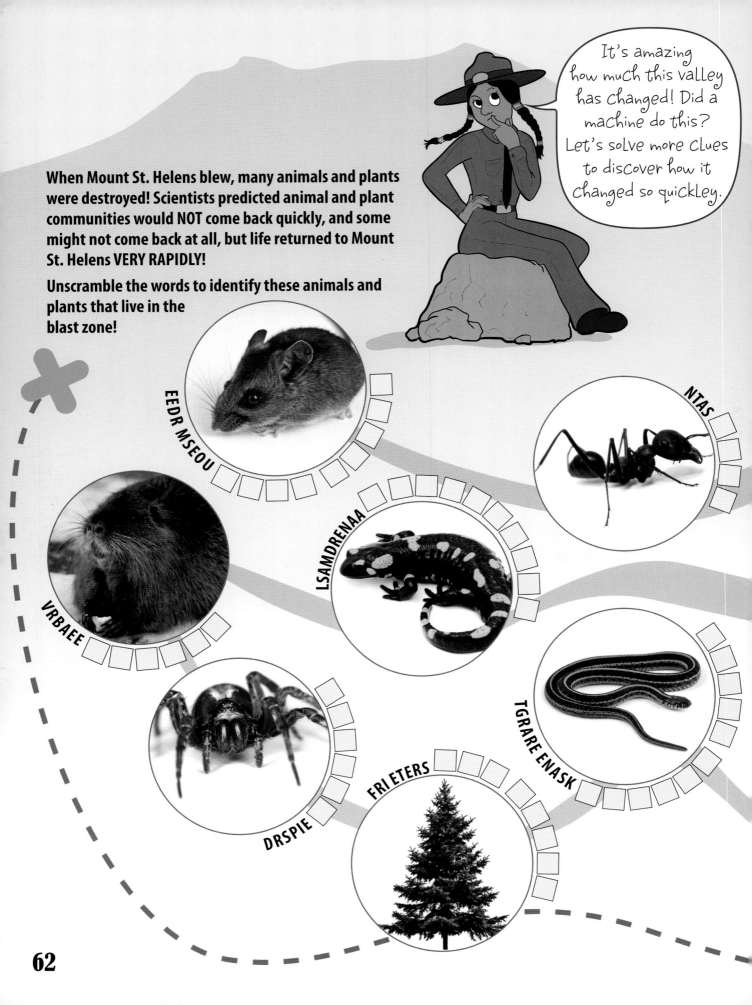

It's amazing how much this valley has changed! Did a machine do this? Let's solve more clues to discover how it changed so quickley.

When Mount St. Helens blew, many animals and plants were destroyed! Scientists predicted animal and plant communities would NOT come back quickly, and some might not come back at all, but life returned to Mount St. Helens VERY RAPIDLY!

Unscramble the words to identify these animals and plants that live in the blast zone!

EEDR MSEOU

NTAS

VRBAEE

LSAMDRENAA

TGRARE ENASK

DRSPIE

FRI ETERS

62

Discovering plant and animal

| | | | | | | | | |
| TA | TI | NE | EN | NA | EN | EI | NE | TA |

in the wasteland was surprising. HOWEVER the parade of life that came to Mount St. Helens in the months and years afterward astounded and shocked scientists!

Spider & Insect Rain!

Parachuting in, and wafting on the wind, millions of spiders and insects, following their normal life cycle, rained from the sky onto the ash-covered earth. Few survived, but these "bug bodies" became food for animals, insects, and spiders, and

| | | | | | | | | |
| TT | EE | NE | AE | NA | TN | NA | ET | EE | NE |

for plants!

Use the square code for these clues!

CIFICAP TEER FRGO

TGRIE EEEBLT

That's one rain I would DEFINITELY use an umbrella for!

GNDROU RRLEQSUI

YOTCEO

UOTRT

KLE

#7

Colorful Colonizers!

Growing on top of bug body buildup, wildflowers like

TN	TI	NT	NA	EA	EE

and fireweed, were some of the first plants to spring up after the eruption were pioneer plants! Red alder, cottonwood, willow, silver fir and other trees also sprang up, pioneering the way for large mammals to return to Mount St. Helens!

ALL you can Eat Buffet!

This bountiful buffet of plants became a tasty treat to elk and other large mammals. Just two years after the eruption, elk returned to Mount St. Helens! Elk began having

				and								
AE	IE	NA	EA	TA	AE	NE	NA	NT	TN	EE	AE	TA

causing the elk herd to grow very large and healthy!

Colonizer plants & animals start a chain of events leading to a healthy ecosystem.

hint Ecosystem is a community of plants, animals, and other organisms living in an area which provides basic survival needs.

Look at this pond! Life is quickly covering up signs of damage from the volcano here! I see another clue envelope on the edge of the pond!

Ponds like this one are also home to the aquatic life now found near Mount St. Helens.

Most people are not allowed to step off of the trails here because plants could be damaged. There is a saying around here. "Plants grow by the inch & die by the foot."

Rangers Jack and Jen brought some tools that will help with the investigation! Use the square code key (on page 59) to discover which tools Ranger Jack brought to study the pond.

1. **EA EI AE EE NN EI EI IT**   _ _ _ _ _ _ _ _ _

2. **NT EE EA TE NA TN**   _ _ _ _ _ _ _

3. **NN EI IE TN TA**   _ _ _ _ _ _

4. **EA EE AE**   _ _ _

5. **TE II AI EE NE II**   _ _ _ _ _ _

Aquatic Life

Use your detective skills to help Ranger Jen and Jack discover the aquatic life living in and near the pond.

Crayfish
Stonefly
Mayfly
Dragonfly
Sculpin

Horse tail
Trout
Caddisfly larvae
Dragonfly nymph
Frog eggs

Pacific tree frog
Water strider
Wolf spider
~~Water boatman~~

H	P	A	C	I	F	I	C	T	R	E	E	F	R	O	G
S	O	Q	P	Z	R	H	E	C	Q	J	O	Y	C	X	H
I	D	E	K	F	L	C	L	R	G	K	I	D	Q	Z	J
S	N	M	K	X	J	M	L	A	F	Y	G	Z	A	M	V
L	Y	E	H	D	W	R	M	Y	L	K	U	D	S	X	E
D	Y	D	R	A	G	O	N	F	L	Y	E	V	N	M	A
U	X	W	I	F	B	M	E	I	S	E	H	D	T	J	V
W	R	N	O	Y	U	N	A	S	Q	Z	E	T	N	O	R
A	G	C	W	M	O	Y	Z	H	Z	U	I	E	V	B	A
T	B	W	A	T	E	R	B	O	A	T	M	A	N	X	L
E	F	X	S	Z	X	V	M	Y	G	R	G	H	P	L	Y
R	D	E	C	V	M	G	M	P	H	O	D	O	T	Q	L
S	B	V	N	M	C	A	A	D	B	U	S	R	I	E	F
T	G	E	U	I	O	X	Y	Z	X	T	A	S	D	O	S
R	L	R	E	D	I	P	S	F	L	O	W	E	N	N	I
I	K	D	U	Z	M	C	G	U	L	F	K	T	E	D	D
D	W	W	Y	E	U	D	B	Y	E	Y	P	A	V	F	D
E	Q	U	H	L	H	L	E	U	V	M	X	I	B	L	A
R	B	I	P	F	R	O	G	E	G	G	S	L	X	P	C
H	S	I	Q	J	V	E	I	U	O	D	Z	X	H	Y	K
A	N	D	R	A	G	O	N	F	L	Y	N	Y	M	P	H

There are pictures on the back of the clue envelope. Both pictures were taken from different angles and different years. See the amazing difference!

This scene went from gray to green very rapidly!

And it was NOT a Giant Green Scene Machine that changed Mount St. Helens after the blast!

What Changed This Scene from Gray to Green?

Research into plants and animal interactions after the eruption has given scientists great information about how to help in other locations where forests are severely damaged. Lots of animal and plant life can once again be seen at Mount St. Helens!

This research gives great insight into how rapidly life recovered after Noah's Flood!

67

Rockin' Ranger

Aquatic Investigator: Discover the Secrets of the Deep!

You Need:

Lake, pond, or stream	Net
Notebook	Magnifying hand lens
Pencil	Plastic bowls (white is the best color)

Investigation Tips:
Water creatures are fragile! Handle with care!
Bring a bag to pick up trash in the area.
Shore may be slippery. Don't fall in!
If water is deep or swift, wear a life jacket.

Directions:

Spy Mission! Locate a pond, stream, or lake.

Eye Spy! Investigate the area around the water.

Sketch Artist! Make a sketch of the area in your notebook.

Peer into the underwater world! Stand quietly and explore the water with your eyes. What do you see?

Collection! Use your dip net to make a small "tornado" in the water. Scoop your net through the tornado across the bottom. Try to capture leaves, twigs, and mud, too!

Inspection! Critters will be camouflaged. Inspect contents of the net closely. Swish it through the water to get out excess mud. (Hint: Use a stick if needed to help look through the contents.)

Fill collection bowls with water! Carefully place water critters into bowl and inspect them with the magnifying lens. Return everything else in the net to the water.

Make a Memory! Sketch a picture of one of your water critters.

Critter ID! See if you can identify these water critters. (Use a pond book or the internet.) Do you see any of the same critters that Ranger Jack and Jen found in the pond at Mount St. Helens?

Home again! Return your critters very gently to their natural habitat.

Rockin' Ranger

Leaf Animal Challenge!

You Need:
Leaves — different colors, shapes, and sizes
Construction paper or poster board
Glue
Crayons or markers
Heavy books
Paper towels

Directions:

Spy Mission! Gather lots of leaves of different colors, shapes, and sizes!

Spy Eyes! Lay out the leaves. Use your super spy imagination to picture an animal shape.

Shape it! Move the leaves around to form the animal shape. Create as many leaf animals as you would like.

Bonding! Glue the animal shape to the paper and set it aside to dry. Add details to your animal with markers or crayons.

Undercover! When the glue is dry, place a paper towel over the picture and heavy books on top.

Book it! Leave the books in place for a few days. The leaves will dry nice and flat.

Optional! Cover your creation with clear lamination to preserve your work of art.

Mystery of the Lost Treasure!

We have solved seven AMAZING mysteries! However, there is still one we haven't solved yet.

How does the eruption of Mount St. Helens help us understand Noah's Flood and earth's history?!

 **hint**

Uncover hidden secrets about Noah's Flood. There is a real treasure at the end.

There's a clue envelope near that log with a treasure map inside!

Solve the treasure map clues by filling in the missing letters. Use this number code if you need it: 1 = a, 2 = b, 3=C and so on.

mystery ranger

When Mount St. Helens rumbled and __lew (2), it left some giant, really big clues! With earthquakes and landslides and a really big blast, the mountain's eruption revealed secrets to the __ast (16). To unlock these secrets of earth's __istory (8), Follow the clues to this strange mystery.

Clue: Quick Change Artist!

Mount St. Helens landscape was QUICKLY changed. In just a few minutes it was __earranged (18)!

Noah's Flood With lots of water and lots of __ud (13), Earth's landscape changed QUICKLY in Noah's Flood.

Clue: Big Deposits!

Mount St. Helens eruption deposited mud, rocks, and __sh (1), Also forming layers of strata, some as quick as a flash.

Noah's Flood moved lots of rock, mud and debris, Depositing layers worldwide and deep in the __ea (19).

Clue: Erosion Power!

Mount St. Helens Mudflows sped down the mountain with might, Their power carved channels and helped streams __nite (21). With very deep canyons formed in nine hours, this new river system showed erosion's __ower (16)!

Noah's Flood caused erosion with full force and power. The earth quickly changed — more every __our (8). Carving canyons, rivers and new landforms too, Noah's Flood left evidence for me and for you.

Unscramble these words to discover some clues! Mount St. Helens and Noah's Flood both had:

Landscapes that changed (yqlciuk) _ _ _ C _ _ _ _!

Large deposits of (umd) _ _ _ and debris.

Powerful (nesorio) _ _ _ _ S _ _ _ _

How is Mount St. Helens like Noah's Flood?

Mount St. Helens

A giant wave caused by the __andslide (12)
Grabbed a million trees and gave them a ride
The trees landed in water with a great big SPLAT!
Spirit Lake was covered with a large log __at (13).

In the years that followed, scientists could see,
what really happened to some of these __rees (20)
These logs soaked up water and started going __own (4)
They landed on the bottom with mud all around.

Buried in layers, these logs made it __ppear (1),
that many forests used to grow here.
The evidence this gave us was valuable information
to understand layering like this in other __ocations (12).

Remember the layering at Specimen Ridge in Yellowstone National Park. It's amazing how much evidence of Noah's Flood you can find when you look!

Noah's Flood

Water covered the planet in a great _atastrophe (3)
The destruction it caused had never been seen.
Like a raging giant, the water smashed and swirled,
grabbing up debris all over the __orld. (23)

Remember Spirit Lake with its large log __at, (13)
Just think of planet earth looking like that!
Did the logs start to sink like they did on Spirit __ake (12)?
Did the flood leave evidence in its giant wake?

Yes, there's lots of evidence for us to see!
Start by looking around the planet for some petrified trees!

Could Noah's Flood have created the Specimen Ridge Layers?

Wow! Noah's Flood did a massive makeover of the earth's surface!

Mount St. Helens

After the eruption it seemed all hope was __one (7).
It would probably be years before life could carry on.

But what scientists found was a great __urprise (19)!
The return of life quickly really opened their eyes!

The return of Life so quickly to Mount St. Helens really shocked scientists!

Noah's Flood

Noah stepped off the ark, and looked all __round (1).
The planet was devastated. Could it rebound?

Trees and plants re-covered the __arth (5).
Animals multiplied in numbers. There were many births!

People spread out and covered the __and (12).
The population grew and started to expand!

Starting with just a few people and animals too,
life recovered quickly. Just look at the zoos!

The Real Treasure!

How do we know about Noah's flood history? Who told us about this amazing __ystery (13)?
Just look around the world with OPEN __yes (5). The landscape shows the flood's story, it's no surprise.
But the words to the story are in God's sacred book, the BIBLE is the TREASURE, the best place to look!

Mount St. Helens is a mini-model of how the earth could have recovered after Noah's Flood!

There's a treasure box! The real treasure is the BIBLE! Now that's something really worth digging into!

Tracking Down the Mystery!
Flood vs. Fire!

I made an exciting discovery in the Treasure Book, THE BIBLE! Look at this!

"In the six hundredth year of Noah's life . . . all the fountains of the great deep were broken up, and the windows of heaven were opened" (Genesis 7:11).

Wow! Not only did Noah's Flood have lots of water, but the earth broke open too! There could have been earthquakes, volcanic eruptions, and tsunamis in Noah's Flood!

So Mount St. Helens and Noah's Flood were both ROCKIN' (with earth breaking) and ROLLING (with lots of water!)
That's the answer to the mystery! The eruption of Mount St. Helens helps us understand Noah's Flood because it can be used as a small scale, mini-model for many events in the flood!

Solve these Crazy Clues to help Ranger Jack and Jen discover which events in Mt. St. Helens eruption were caused by water!

[👂 -a] + ↑↑ + tion = _ _ _ _ _ _ _ _ _ (BOOM! Water vapor helped cause this!)

[Gi + 🐜] [🌊] = _ _ _ _ _] WAVE ON [＼ – ear + irit = **S P I R I T**] L + [🎂 –C = _ _ _ _

De + [🍲 – t] + sit + ion = _ _ _ _ _ _ _ _ _ _ _ (Some deposits were laid down by water.)

E + [🌹 – e] + ion = _ _ _ _ _ _ _ _

74

Seven Amazing Mysteries!

What does Mount St. Helens have to do with Noah's Flood? Investigate a little more!

When Mount St. Helens erupted in a HUGE explosion in 1980, some AWESOME and WONDERFUL mysteries were created that remind us of how fast God created the world, AND how quickly He rearranged it after Noah's flood!

1. Mount St. Helens landscape was totally transformed in **JUST 3–4 Minutes!**

2. Steam explosion pits with rills and gullies formed in **JUST 5 days!**

3. Twenty-five feet of layers were deposited in **JUST 3 hours!** (Later becoming rock!)

4. A WHOLE river system formed in **JUST 9 hours!**

5. Logs on Spirit Lake sank and were buried on the bottom in different layers of sediment giving the appearance of many forests in **JUST 10 years!**

6. Canyons were formed in **JUST 5 months!**

7. Plant and animal life recovered quickly! Elk returned in **JUST 2 years!**

Mysteries of Mount St. Helens Word Search

Use your detective skills to discover the hidden words from the puzzle.

~~Animals~~	Eruption	River System
Ash	God	Spirit Lake
Canyons	Landscape	Steam Pits
Creation	Layers	Volcano
Elk	Logs	
Erosion	Mysteries	

```
M G S F C P G W G Y E L A K S
C O L E S A G Y O S O T Y J T
A E U S I N I M S T J G Y S I
N N L N E R U P T I O N S U P
Y P I K T S E E A S H P U R M
O S J M G S R T N D I G S I A
N L R O A O T O S R Y O E V E
S R L E S L I H I Y R D J E T
V W R I Y T S T E F M R K R S
J O O S A A L E Q L M B Z S S
V N L E U A L R B W E R C Y W
L D R F K F U B K W C N C S U
M C L E P A C S D N A L S T X
D I N F W N X D C C V U C E I
O N A C L O V H Y E Y L B M J
```

75

LARGEST ROCK N' ROLL IN RECORDED HISTORY!	The 5.1 earthquake in the eruption triggered the largest recorded landslide in history!
NEW VOLCANO DANGER DISCOVERED!	Geologists had discovered a new threat from volcanoes — giant landslides!
A GIANT'S FIERY BREATH!	Blasting out of the mountain toward the north at supersonic speed, a fiery hot flow of gas mixed with stone exploded across the landscape toppling trees and killing most wildlife in about a 200 square mile area.
SOMETHING ASTONISH-ING IN THE BLAST CLOUD!	The blast cloud also had something mysterious in it! About 90 percent of the blast cloud contained — superheated water!
A REALLY WEIRD VOLCANO!	No liquid lava flowed from the volcano in the eruption, but it was still very dangerous — 57 people lost their lives in the eruption.
A VOLCANIC TSUNAMI!	Part of the landslide smashed into Spirit Lake, creating a giant water wave 860 feet tall!
AN ELEVATOR LAKE!	Part of the giant landslide settled into Spirit Lake, raising the floor of the lake by 300 feet!
A MUSHROOM IN THE SKY!	Very quickly after the lateral blast, a vertical explosion of ash shot 12 miles into the sky, creating a mushroom-shaped ash cloud!
LIGHTNING BOLTS THROWN FROM THE SKY!	Whirling and swirling, the ash cloud created lightning, which bolted from the sky, starting many forest fires! Most quickly extinguished be-cause the forest was so wet.
TURNING DAYLIGHT INTO DARK!	The ash cloud traveled many miles and reached Yakima and Spokane, Washington, a few hours after the blast. The ash was so thick in the sky that it blocked most of the sunlight! Streetlights came on and stayed on for the rest of the day!
A WORLD TRAVELER!	Ash from Mount St. Helens took just two weeks to travel all the way around the world! Some of the very fine ash stayed in the atmosphere for years!
FALLING FROM THE SKY!	The estimated volume of ash that settled from the sky was enough to cover a football field 150 miles deep!
ASH TO CASH!	Some people turned the ash into sculptures or pieces of art.
A WHALE INSIDE THE VOLCANO!	A strange shape appeared inside the crater in 2004! Magma broke though the surface and started building another dome in the crater. Some of the magma solidified into the shape of a whale! Scientists named this new part of the dome, the "Whaleback."
A SPIDER ON THE WHALEBACK INSIDE THE VOLCANO!	In order to monitor the volcano, scientists placed a scientific unit called a "spider," on top of the Whaleback in 2005. The "spider" didn't survive long. In just 36 hours it was destroyed by an explosion inside the crater. Poor "spider"!
A STEGASAURUS IN THE VOLCANO!	In 2005, shaking and quaking changed the shape of the "whaleback"! It looked like the back of a stegosaurus — a dinosaur with bony plates of armor along its spine.
A MOUNTAIN WITH A BELLYACHE!	Scientists placed more "spiders" in the crater to continue to monitor this mountain with a rumble in its belly!

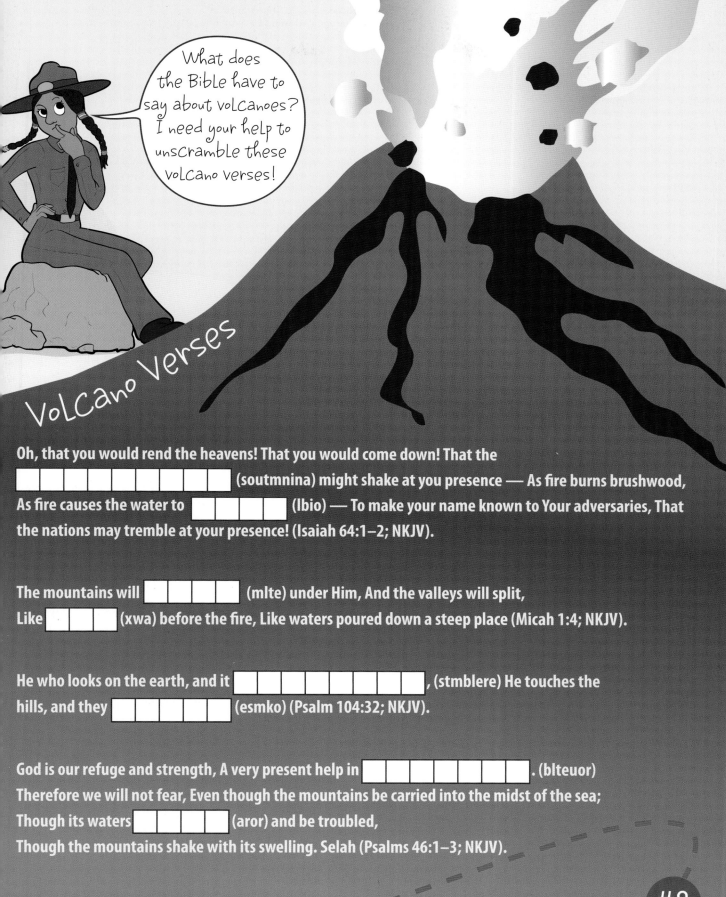

Volcano Verses

Oh, that you would rend the heavens! That you would come down! That the _____ (soutmnina) might shake at your presence — As fire burns brushwood, As fire causes the water to _____ (lbio) — To make your name known to Your adversaries, That the nations may tremble at your presence! (Isaiah 64:1–2; NKJV).

The mountains will _____ (mlte) under Him, And the valleys will split, Like _____ (xwa) before the fire, Like waters poured down a steep place (Micah 1:4; NKJV).

He who looks on the earth, and it _____, (stmblere) He touches the hills, and they _____ (esmko) (Psalm 104:32; NKJV).

God is our refuge and strength, A very present help in _____. (blteuor) Therefore we will not fear, Even though the mountains be carried into the midst of the sea; Though its waters _____ (aror) and be troubled, Though the mountains shake with its swelling. Selah (Psalms 46:1–3; NKJV).

#8

Danger on the Mountain!

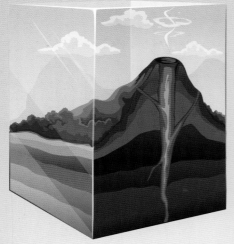

SMOKE SIGNALS! God began the eruption by first touching the mountain gently so that it began to smoke. People came from all over to see this great event! There were scientists, news media, photographers, people who were just curious, and even government agents! They wondered how soon people would have to evacuate their homes. How far would the explosion reach?

EXTREME DANGER! As the mountain developed a HUGE bulge, the governor of Washington, Dixie Lee Ray, had roadblocks set up to protect people to keep them from going too close! They did not like it! They wanted to go to their homes and get their things. The governor did let them go to their homes for a few hours the day before the blast, May 17, but they were in EXTREME DANGER!! They were even supposed to go back the next day, but on May 18, the mountain ERUPTED WITH FURY!

Discover the amazing rescue plan that can save you from a danger even more extreme than the eruption of a volcano.

HE DID NOT LISTEN! One of the people who did not listen to the warnings to leave before the eruption was Harry Truman (not the president.) He owned a tourist lodge at Mount St. Helens near Spirit Lake. It was a beautiful place — a paradise! He was 83 years old, and had lived there a long time. He did not want to leave! Even school children wrote to him and asked him to leave the mountain, but he said, "There is not enough material there to come this far, and it will go the other direction if it is going to blow."

A BAD CHOICE! Harry Truman did not believe the blast would hurt him. Unfortunately, when the eruption occurred, he and everything he owned was buried 150 feet under the new Spirit Lake.

MESSAGE FROM THE MOUNTAIN! The danger of the eruption at Mount St. Helens was EXTREME! However, there is a BIGGER DANGER that we should know about! It is the danger of SIN! Sin separates us from God! The Bible says, "For all have sinned" (Romans 3:23). Everyone sins, so everyone is in EXTREME DANGER from sin! What can we do? Don't worry! There is a way to be rescued from this EXTREME DANGER of sin!

Content used with permission from *When God Spoke Through Nature's Fury* by Doris Anderson; © Mount St. Helens Creation Information Center, Silverlake, WA.

WARNING! Extreme danger of sin ahead! Follow the eternal rescue plan and you can be saved!

Rescue From Danger!

A long time ago there was a warning God gave about the Flood. Only Noah and his family listened to God's warning, and they were the only people saved on the ark.

Thankfully, most people listened to the warnings about the eruption at Mount St. Helens, and their lives were saved. Yet there is a danger we are all warned about even today... SIN!

The Bible shows us that "the wages of sin is death, but the gift of God is eternal life in Christ Jesus our Lord" (Romans 6:23 NKJV). The EXTREME DANGER of sin has put EVERYONE in DANGER of being forever separated from God!

However, God loves you so much that He does not want you to be separated from Him. He made a way for your sins to be forgiven so that you can one day live with Him in heaven! "God so loved the world that He gave His only begotten Son, that whoever believes in Him should not perish but have everlasting life" (John 3:16 NKJV).

If you are willing to repent (turn from your sin) and believe that Jesus died for you and rose again, simply ask Him to save you from your sin. If you're not sure how to pray, you can use the RESCUE PRAYER (below) to guide you. But it's okay to use your own words when you talk to God. He's always ready to listen!

DANGER

Rescue Prayer

Dear Jesus, I know I'm a sinner, and I believe You took the punishment for my sins. Please forgive me for my sin. Now please come into my life. In Jesus' name, Amen.

If you have accepted God's rescue, you are SAVED, and nothing can take that away, not even the BIGGEST VOLCANO BLAST in the world!

Mystery Ranger Volcano Jokes (An eruption of fun!)

1. A volcano is a mountain with hiccups!

2. What did one volcano say to the other? I lava you!

3. How did the volcano see at night? It had a lava lamp.
   Submitted by: Britt Fugler

4. What did the volcano do when he got angry? He blew his top!
   Submitted by: Brad Williams

5. What do you call a cute volcano? Lavable! (lovable!)

6. What did the mama volcano say to the baby volcano? "Don't erupt while I'm talking!"

7. What happens when geese land in a volcano? They cook their own goose!

8. Why shouldn't you tell a volcano a joke? It might crack up laughing.
   Submitted by: Nathanael and Noelia

9. Why shouldn't you get a volcano mad? It might blow its stack.
   Submitted by: Nathanael and Noelia

10. Why is a volcano like a health spa? It provides a hot mud bath.
    Submitted by: Nathanael and Noelia

11. What kind of plants grow in hot lava? Flow-ers.
    Submitted by: Nathanael and Noelia

Check off each mystery as you solve it! To become an Official Mystery Ranger, solve all the mysteries, complete 2 Rockin' Ranger Activities and two Mystery Ranger Missions!

- ☐ Mystery of the Vanishing Volcano!
- ☐ Mystery of Exploding Ice and Snow!
- ☐ Mystery of the Cliff of Secrets!
- ☐ Mystery of the Menacing Mudslinger
- ☐ Mystery of the Floating Forest!
- ☐ Mystery of the Mighty Canyon Carvers!
- ☐ Mystery of the Green Scene Machine!

To download your reward, go to: thenaturetour.com

Complete two of these Missions!

- » Make a poster to teach someone about the Mysteries of Mount St. Helens.
- » Share the Eternal Life Rescue Plan with one person.
- » Memorize two Volcano Verses.
- » Pick up two bags of litter from your neighborhood or a park.
- » Help your parents with a project around the house.
- » Create your own projects or games to teach about the Mount St. Helens Mysteries. Write them here:

_____

_____

Mystery Ranger Answer Key

Page 3

3. What is the abbreviation for Mount? **MT**

4. What does St. in "Mount St. Helens" stand for? **SAINT**

Page 4

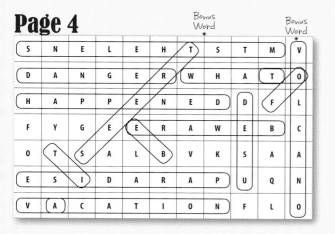

Page 7

Danger lurked quietly under Mount St. Helens, a paradise of clear **LAKES** and beautiful forests full of **WILDLIFE**. Unaware of danger, people vacationed and worked on the mountain.

Suddenly, Mount St. Helens woke up! Thousands of minor earthquakes signaled magma movement! Pushing with mighty force, magma created a giant **BULGE** 450 feet tall, near the top of the mountain on the **NORTH** side.

As the **MONSTROUS** bulge filled with fiery hot melted rock called **MAGMA**, it grew. snow and ice on top of the mountain melted and seeped into tiny **CRACKS** created by the minor earthquakes.

Page 8

On May 18, 1980, a very powerful **EARTHQUAKE** shook Mount St. Helens, causing the north side bulge of the mountain to start to plunge into the valley below.

As the bulge slid off, super hot water inside the mountain exploded to **STEAM** causing the clay layers inside the mountain to be very **SLIPPERY**. Zoom! Zoom! Zoom! In three sections, the bulge, along with the top on quarter, and then half of the mountain's insides slid off into the largest **LANDSLIDE** in recorded history!

Page 9

When the ground slid away, it was like shaking up a bottle of soda, and taking off the cap! It released the **PRESSURE** inside the mountain with huge lateral (sideways) and vertical blasts!

In just **THREE** to **FOUR** minutes, most of the damage to the area was done! The mountain was disfigured beyond recognition. The valley was filled with the landslide, and forest as large as a big **CITY** were destroyed.

The main eruption continued for **NINE** hours, forming an ash cloud over 12 miles high!

Mount St. Helens did not look like it did before the eruption! The mountain and area to the north looked like the surface of the **MOON**.

Wow! Scientists were amazed that so much land cound be changed so **QUICKLY**.

Page 11

Multiple lava flows build up to create the wide, gently sloping cone of a shield volcano. Most shield volcanoes erupt **NON-EXPLOSIVELY**. This type of eruption can destroy **PROPERTY**, but rarely causes death or injury. Mauna Loa volcano in Hawaii which rises over 30,000 feet above the ocean floor, is a shield volcano.

Composite volcanoes, usually very steep and tall, are made of alternating layers of lava, ash, and rock fragments. They tend to erupt **EXPLOSIVELY** because the magma is too stiff for gasses to escape easily. Pressure builds as trapped gases expand until it is released in a violent eruption very **DANGEROUS** to people and property. Composite volcanoes are also known as stratovolcanoes. Mount Fuji in Japan is a composite volcano.

Mount St. Helens erupted explosively. It is a **COMPOSITE** volcano.

Page 12 & 13

Ah ha! There was an explosive eruption at 10. MT ST HELENS because it's a 2. COMPOSITE VOLCANO. That's why there was a lot of 1.DANGER! Many scientists used to think this much change to a landscape took million of years. But most of this change took just THREE to FOUR 6.MINUTES!

Did the volcano really 5. VANISH? No, it was still there. But it looked TOTALLY different than before the 8. ERUPTION. It was no longer a vacation paradise. The HUGE debris avalanche left the mountain 1,314 feet shorter, with a HUGE horseshoe shaped 9.CRATER on top.

How far did the 3.BLAST reach? It reached up to 17 miles on the 7.NORTH side

1. TREE (4)
Removal Zone
(No trees left)

2. BLOW DOWN (12) Zone
(Trees blown over)

3. SCORCH (11) Zone
(Trees were standing but scorched.)

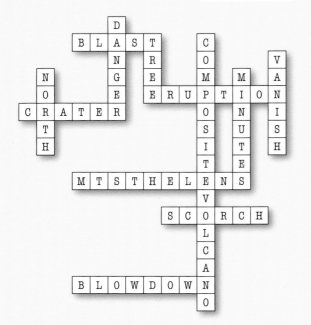

Page 14 & 15

Unscramble words

(b r C a n o x D o i e d i) CARBON DIOXIDE

This volcano model represents a (dsiehl) SHIELD volcano.

Magma, which is melted (rcko) ROCK inside of a volcano, is called (aalv) LAVA when it reaches the earth's (srfaceu) SURFACE!

Page 16

The bubbles in the bottle are like GAS bubbles rising out of the magma of a volcano. They are TRAPPED against the lid, and the pressure builds.

When the cap was taken off the bottle, and the PRESSURE was released, what happened?

This is a great comparison to what happened at Mount St. Helens. When the LAND slid off the top of the MOUNTAIN, the pressure was released, and there was a gigantic BLAST!

Page 17

All of these volcano models are a little different from real (noeslovca) VOLCANOES.

In this volcano model, (bonrac xdioeid) CARBON DIOXIDE caused the eruption.

In most volcanoes, (twrea vproa) WATER VAPOR is the main gas causing most eruptions, not carbon dioxide.

Page 18
HARNESS AND ROPE

Page 20

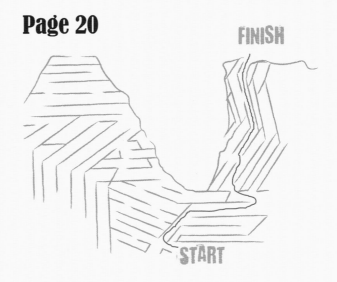

Page 21-23

Clue #1 - LANDSLIDES

Clue #2 - HOT ASH

Clue #3 - STEAM, EXPLOSIONS

Clue #4 - PUMICE, RILLS, GULLIES

Clue #5 - BADLANDS

Clue #6 - EROSION, SEDIMENTARY, PINNACLES

Clue #7 - RAIN, PLANTS, SEDIMENTS

Clue #8 - VOLCANIC, EXPLOSIONS, LOOSE, PLANTS, GRAVITY

Clue #9 - CATASTROPHE, NOAH'S FLOOD

Page 24

This evidence demonstrates that it did NOT have to take HUNDREDS or THOUSANDS of YEARS for the BADLANDS of South DAKOTA to form!

Page 25

The 5.1 earthquake at Mount St. Helens caused three (desllnaids) LANDSLIDES which joined together to form one giant landslide!

The giant landslide carried huge amounts of (eic) ICE and (wons) SNOW!

The buried ice and snow were covered with very hot volcanic (sah) ASH.

The buried ice and snow quickly flashed to (tmesa) STEAM.

When the steam built up pressure too quickly it caused large (spoxelnsio) EXPLOSIONS!

These steam explosions created steam explosion (stpi) PITS .

The force of (ygatriv) GRAVITY helped carve rills and gullies into the sides of the pits.

The pumice plain now had huge pits, and looked similar to an area in South Dakota called the (dslBaand) BADLANDS.

The steam explosion pits at Mount St. Helens looked like badlands topography in only (efvi) FIVE days.

Page 27

Water can wash away small amounts of soil, creating very small channels called RILLS.

If water continues to flow in rill channels, deeper ditches called GULLIES will form.

AMAZING! WATER erosion is usually what forms rills and gullies. HOWEVER, at Mount St. Helens, rills and gullies were formed by STEAM explosions and GRAVITY in just five days!

Page 28

How fast did pyroclastic flows create 200 layers on this cliff?

Page 29

Created by melting snow from an eruption, this mighty mudflow muscled its way down the mountain covering and carving through past avalanche DEBRIS. Like icing on a cake, it covered the cliff of secrets, forming the TOP deposit.

A raging HOT fiery cloud of gas, rocks, and ash called a PYROCLASTIC flow stormed at hurricane speed down the volcano, creating over 200 layers in just three hours!

Volcanic lightening, triggered by swirling ash, flashed all around! Tephra (any kind of ASH and ROCK ejected from a volcano through the air) spewed from Mt. St. Helens for nine hours, creating this 30 foot deep deposit.

Page 30

FLOOD GEOLOGISTS suspect the TAPEATS LAYERS at the GRAND CANYON were formed during NOAH'S FLOOD!

Page 31

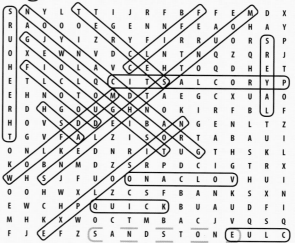

Page 33

A hot, fast-moving mixture of (sha) **ASH**, pumice, (rcko) **ROCK** fragments, and gas formed during explosive eruptions is called a (citsalcoryp) **PYROCLASTIC** flow.

The word PYROCLASTIC , comes from the Greek word *pyro* meaning (rife) **FIRE** and klastos meaning (nebokr) **BROKEN**.

Page 34-36

There was a **MUDSLINGING BATTLE** here!

Part of the landslide (about 25 percent) slammed into **SPIRIT LAKE**.

The rest of the landslide (75 percent) pushed and shoved its way through the valley, covering up 14 miles of the North Fork of the **TOUTLE RIVER**.

Melting ice and snow flowed rapidly over the landslide, gobbling up **SOIL** rocks, and trees from the landslide.

The menacing mudflow roared down the valley, snatching up everything in its path! Huge piles of cut **LOGS** were sucked into the muddy mass when it smashed into logging camps.

It ripped and roared for many miles until it reached the **COLUMBIA** River where it settled down as a humongous mud pie, filling the river channel with so much mud that it was too shallow for big boats.

Page 37

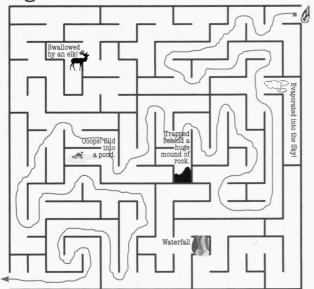

Page 38-41

MIGHTY MUDFLOW is here! With a quake and shake, another eruption melted **SNOW** in the crater of Mount St. Helens, and a second HUGE MUDFLOW was born.

The MIGHTY MUDFLOW thundered down the mountain with speed, power, and lot's of mud. It was 20 miles long and ready to pack a punch through the lumpy landslide on the **TOUTLE RIVER**.

The landslide held its ground, but very quickly MIGHTY MUDFLOW swept away massive amounts of jumbled **ROCK**, **ASH**, and dirt.

The MIGHTY MUDFLOW had used its super erosion powers and carved a **CANYON** in the new river system that was 140 deep in just 9 hours.

It was nicknamed "The Little **GRAND** Canyon" because it appeared to be 1/40th the size of the Grand Canyon in Arizona!

For two years the water level at **SPIRIT LAKE** was getting higher!

A temporary pipeline was used to pump water out of the lake for 28 months while a 1.5 mile drainage **TUNNEL** was built through a ridge to Spirit Lake. They used a machine they nicknamed "The Mole" to dig the tunnel. It looked like a giant **DENTIST DRILL**.

The massive amount of water pumped out of Spirit Lake by the temporary pipeline for 28 months eroded a deep canyon named **ENGINEERS CANYON**.

Page 42

HOW LONG DID IT TAKE THESE LANDFORMS TO DEVELOP?

Engineer's Canyon   **28 MONTHS**

Little Grand Canyon   **9 HOURS**

North Fork Toutle River System   **9 HOURS** new system

Page 48

Estimated age of tree **BETWEEN 19-21 YEARS**

Page 50

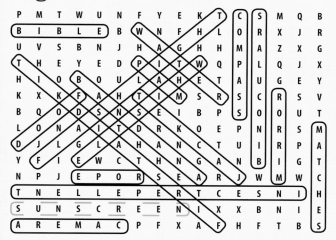

Page 51

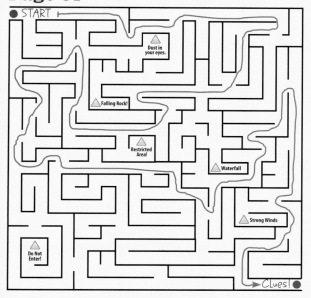

Page 52

seeatqhkrua **EARTHQUAKES**

irenghaewt **WEATHERING**

gwionrg alav eomd **GROWING LAVA DOME**

eci wnso esplolac **ICE or SNOW COLLAPSE**

Page 54-56

STEP CANYON and LOOWIT CANYON

FIVE MONTHS

MUDFLOWS and PYROCLASTIC FLOWS

AVALANCHE DEBRIS and SOLID ROCK

FIVE MONTHS

LOWER LOOWIT CANYON

CAVITATION and PLUCKING

Page 59-60

Hike through the Hummocks and you will see another clue to this MYSTERY.

The LANDSLIDE surged with SUPER SPEED 14 miles down the North Fork of the Toutle River. It filled the valley to an average thickness of 150 feet.

Mounds of rock from the volcano, called HUMMOCKS stick up like huge beached whales in the landslide deposit.

Page 61

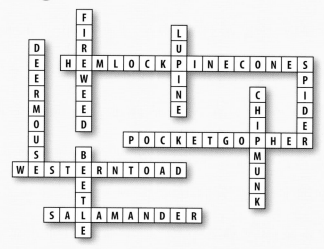

Page 62-64

eedr mseou - **DEER MOUSE** vrbaee - **BEAVER**

lsamdrenaa - **SALAMANDER** drspie - **SPIDER**

tgrare enask - **GARTER SNAKE** ntas - **ANTS**

fri eters - **FIR TREES** yotceo - **COYOTE**

cificap teer frgo - **PACIFIC TREE FROG**

tgrie eeeblt - **TIGER BEETLE** uotrt - **TROUT**

gndrou rrleqsui - **GROUND SQUIRREL**

kle - **ELK**

Discovering plant and animal SURVIVORS in the wasteland was surprising.

Few survived, but these "bug bodies" became food for animals, insects, and spiders, and FERTILIZER for plants!

Growing on top of bug body buildup, wildflowers like LUPINE and fireweed, were some of the first plants to spring up after the eruption, were pioneer plants!

Elk began having TWINS and TRIPLETS causing the elk herd to grow very large and healthy!

Page 65

1. EA EI AE EE NN EI EI IT   **NOTEBOOK**
2. NT EE EA TE NA TN   **PENCIL**
3. NN EI IE TN TA   **BOWLS**
4. EA EE AE   **NET**
5. TE II AI EE NE II   **CAMERA**

Page 66

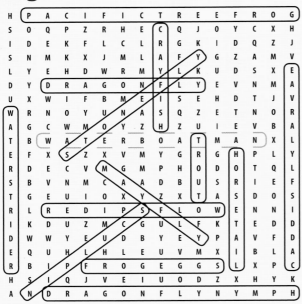

Page 71

Rearranged ⇨ Mud

Ash ⇨ Sea

Unite, Power ⇨ Hour

Landscapes that changed (yqlciuk) **QUICKLY!**

Large deposits of (umd) **MUD** and debris.

Powerful (nesorio) **EROSION**

Page 72-73

Landslide (12)	Catastrophe (3)	Around (1)
Mat (13)	World (23)	Earth (5)
Trees (20)	Mat (13)	Land (12)
Down (4)	Lake (12)	Mystery (13)
Appear (1)	Gone (7)	Eyes (5)
Locations (12)	Surprise (19)	

Page 74

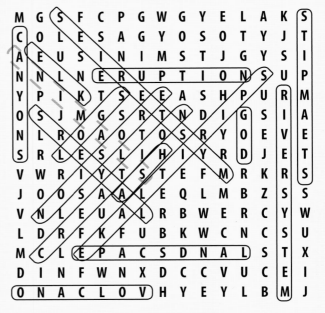

Page 75

Page 77

Oh, that you would rend the heavens! That you would come down! That the MOUNTAINS (soutmnina) might shake at you presence — As fire burns brushwood, As fire causes the water to BOIL (lbio) — To make your name known to Your adversaries, That the nations may tremble at your presence! (Isaiah 64:1–2; NKJV).

The mountains will MELT (mlte) under Him, And the valleys will split, Like WAX (xwa) before the fire, Like waters poured down a steep place (Micah 1:4; NKJV).

He who looks on the earth, and it TREMBLES, (stmblere) He touches the hills, and they SMOKE (esmko) (Psalm 104:32; NKJV).

God is our refuge and strength, A very present help in TROUBLE. (blteuor) Therefore we will not fear, Even though the mountains be carried into the midst of the sea; Though its waters ROAR (aror) and be troubled,Though the mountains shake with its swelling. Selah (Psalms 46:1–3; NKJV).

GOD'S DESIGN
FOR SCIENCE SERIES

EXPLORE GOD'S WORLD OF SCIENCE WITH THESE FUN CREATION-BASED SCIENCE COURSES

GOD'S DESIGN FOR LIFE
GRADES 3-8

Learn all about biology as students study the intricacies of life science through human anatomy, botany, and zoology.

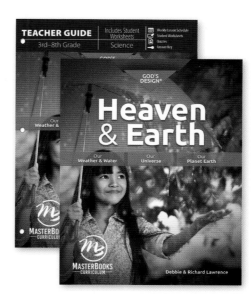

GOD'S DESIGN FOR HEAVEN & EARTH
GRADES 3-8

Explore God's creation of the land and skies with geology, astronomy, and meteorology.

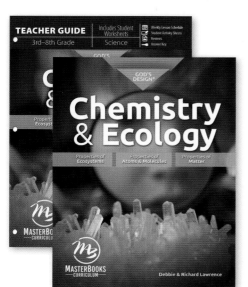

GOD'S DESIGN FOR CHEMISTRY & ECOLOGY
GRADES 3-8

Discover the exciting subjects of chemistry and ecology through studies of atoms, molecules, matter, and ecosystems.

GOD'S DESIGN FOR THE PHYSICAL WORLD
GRADES 3-8

Study introductory physics and the mechanisms of heat, machines, and technology with this accessible course.